Black Abolitionism

The Bishop Henry McNeal Turner/Sojourner Truth Series in Black Religion

Editor: Dwight N. Hopkins

The purpose of this series is to encourage the development of biblical, historical, theological, ethical, and pastoral works that analyze the role of the churches and other religious movements in the liberation struggles of black women and men in the United States, particularly the poor, and their relationship to struggles in the Third World.

Named after Bishop Henry McNeal Turner (1843-1915) and Sojourner Truth (1797?-1883), the series reflects the spirit of these two visionaries and witnesses for the black struggle for liberation. Bishop Turner was a churchman, a political figure, a missionary, and a pan-Africanist. Sojourner Truth was an illiterate former slave who championed black emancipation, women's rights, and the liberating spirit of the gospel.

Previously published in the Turner Series:

1. *For My People* by James H. Cone
2. *Black and African Theologies* by Josiah U. Young
3. *Troubling Biblical Waters* by Cain Hope Felder
4. *Black Theology USA and South Africa* by Dwight N. Hopkins
5. *Empower the People* by Theodore Walker, Jr.
6. *A Common Journey* by George C.L. Cummings
7. *Dark Symbols, Obscure Signs* by Riggins R. Earl, Jr.
8. *A Troubling in My Soul* by Emilie Townes
9. *The Black Christ* by Kelly Brown Douglas

In the Turner/Truth Series:

10. *Christianity on Trial* by Mark L. Chapman
11. *Were You There?* by David Emmanuel Goatley
12. *My Sister, My Brother* by Karen Baker-Fletcher and Garth (Kasimu) Baker-Fletcher
13. *Embracing the Spirit: Womanist Perspectives on Hope, Salvation, and Transformation* by Emilie M. Townes, editor
14. *Exorcizing Evil: A Womanist Perspective on the Spirituals* by Cheryl A. Kirk-Duggan
15. *Power in the Blood? The Cross in the African American Experience* by JoAnne Marie Terrell
16. *Resurrection Song: African-American Spirituality* by Flora Wilson Bridges

The Bishop Henry McNeal Turner/Sojourner Truth Series
in Black Religion, Volume XVII

Black Abolitionism

A Quest for Human Dignity

Beverly Eileen Mitchell

ORBIS ⊕ BOOKS

Maryknoll, New York 10545

Founded in 1970, Orbis Books endeavors to publish works that enlighten the mind, nourish the spirit, and challenge the conscience. The publishing arm of the Maryknoll Fathers and Brothers, Orbis seeks to explore the global dimensions of the Christian faith and mission, to invite dialogue with diverse cultures and religious traditions, and to serve the cause of reconciliation and peace. The books published reflect the views of their authors and do not represent the official position of the Maryknoll Society. To learn more about Maryknoll and Orbis Books, please visit our website at www.maryknoll.org.

Copyright © 2005 by Beverly Eileen Mitchell

Published by Orbis Books, Maryknoll, NY 10545-0308
Manufactured in the United States of America
Manuscript editing and typesetting by Joan Weber Laflamme

Library of Congress Cataloging-in-Publication Data

Mitchell, Beverly Eileen.
  Black abolitionism : a quest for human dignity / by Beverly Eileen Mitchell.
    p. cm. — (Bishop Henry McNeal Turner/Sojourner Truth series in Black religion ; v. 17)
  Includes index.
  ISBN 1-57075-591-4 (pbk.)
  1. Human rights. 2. Dignity. 3. Slavery—United States. 4. African American abolitionists. 5. Racism—United States. I. Title. II. Series.
 JC571.M58 2005
 326'.8'08996073—dc22

                                2004020071

*In memory of Charlotte Forten Grimke (1837–1914),
whose journals inspired this project.*

*To all those who have given their lives
in defense of the dignity of the marginalized.*

Contents

PART III
THE ENEMY OF THE QUEST

Acknowledgments

I am grateful to Wesley Theological Seminary for the sabbatical that gave me the time to devote to this project. In particular, I want to express my appreciation to Bruce C. Birch, academic dean, for his interest and encouragement. I am also grateful to the faculty members of Wesley Theological Seminary for their helpful comments on three chapters of the manuscript that were discussed during a stimulating faculty study session. I also want to express my gratitude to several persons who graciously agreed to read an earlier draft of the manuscript and offered good suggestions: Deborah van Broekhoven; Ann K. Riggs; and my colleagues at Wesley: Douglas M. Strong, Josiah U. Young, III, and Mary Clark Moschella. I would also like to thank Quentin Graham for his wise counsel along the way.

Additionally, I am indebted to the editor of this series, Dwight N. Hopkins, for his insightful critique of the manuscript and to my editor at Orbis Books, Susan Perry, for her patience and editorial assistance. I would also like to express a word of appreciation to Joan Laflamme and Catherine Costello for their queries and attention to details. Their contributions helped to refine the finished product.

I am most appreciative of the love and support of my family. In particular, I am grateful to my parents, Marvin and Edwina Mitchell, for the values they instilled in me and the daily prayers they have offered in my behalf. I thank my sisters, Joyce and Janice, for the cherished friendship we have shared all our lives. I am truly blessed.

Introduction

At its core, black abolitionism was a quest for recognition of the worth and human dignity of African Americans. The question of the full humanity of blacks was at the root of their struggle for emancipation and restoration to their divinely conferred status as full human beings. Black abolitionists not only fought for the independence of blacks from bondage, but they also sought to ensure that those of African descent would become full participants in American society. They did not assume that once the slave trade ended and slavery was abolished in the land, the problems that had assailed them in America would be completely resolved. They understood that emancipation was only the *first* step toward their ultimate goal. Thus, emancipation from slavery was viewed as a necessary but insufficient step in the struggle for freedom and justice in America.

Unfortunately, the instincts of black abolitionists on this score were correct. As subsequent history shows, the fight for emancipation was not the end of their struggle, for blacks endured a harsh backlash after the failure of Reconstruction. They also suffered the indignities of Jim Crow and increased legalization of segregation in all areas of their lives in the North and more particularly in the South. Moreover, the unfinished work of the abolitionist movement of the nineteenth century would lead to further attempts to secure justice in the modern civil rights movement of the 1950s and 1960s. Although this latter movement resulted in the acquisition of certain sociopolitical rights, the spiritual or theological goal of the abolitionists' struggle in America–*full* recognition of their dignity and worth as human beings–remained unfulfilled.

The outcomes of both the abolitionist and the modern civil rights movements have demonstrated that legal, social, political, and economic gains toward full equality remain insufficient for full relief in African Americans' struggle for a meaningful, productive life in the United States. What was and is still needed is a frontal attack on the ideology of racism or white supremacy. Recognition of the power of white supremacy to thwart both the Christian gospel message and democratic ideals, which served as the foundation for the American experiment, is needed to help clarify the nature of the challenge toward full equality in America for African Americans. The history of blacks in America in light of the ideology of white supremacy illustrates the degree of difficulty that black Americans have had in trying to achieve their goal of equal justice. It is to be hoped that the insights we can gain regarding this unfulfilled quest can help us to try fresh, new measures leading toward that fulfillment without incurring losses from the gains that blacks have made already in their journey toward justice in America.

However, before we can draw any meaning from the insights gained from examining the quest of the black abolitionists, we must first examine the particular features of the institution of slavery as it developed in North America, investigate the assumptions of white and black abolitionists to determine how and why they differed, and explore the nature of the underlying ideology of white supremacy as it shaped the institution of slavery and adversely affected the success of abolitionism. With regard to these three dimensions of the study of the quest of black abolitionism, I make three claims:

1. The nature of slavery in North America was distinctively different from previous forms of slavery in other civilizations. Slavery in North America was designed, categorically and systematically, to *dehumanize* blacks who were forced to serve under this system.

2. Although whites and blacks did work together in abolitionist activities, they often had different assumptions about what emancipation would entail, the potential of blacks to win full participation in American society, and the degree and lengths to which blacks should go to achieve that goal. One could not assume that one who professed to be an abolitionist also recognized that blacks ought to have the right to full participation in American society.

3. The ideology of white supremacy was so pervasive in both the North and the South that the failure to address racism theologically,

politically, and socially led to the ultimate failure of blacks to achieve full justice in American society.

An examination of the writings of black abolitionists in light of these three dimensions leads to two important conclusions about the nature of black abolitionism which distinguish it from white abolitionism. First, black abolitionism and white abolitionism were distinct, parallel movements, even though blacks and whites often participated in biracial organizations to work for the abolition of slavery. Second, without recognition of the full human dignity of blacks, emancipation from slavery (and its economic, social, and political effects) would remain incomplete.

The institution of American slavery emerged as a profitable economic enterprise, and when its profitability became evident, greed perpetuated the system. Out of this economic profitability elaborate philosophical, theological, and pseudo-scientific justifications were sought to support the system, and social and political measures were used to sustain it. It can be argued that if slavery had not proven to be economically profitable, the elaborate measures used to support it would not have been advanced. This is not to say that Americans would have been immune to ethnocentrism or even some form of racism, but the virulence of this malady would not have been so great if slavery had not been economically profitable in the beginning. Racism (or more precisely, white supremacy) in the form we find in the United States took on a life of its own; it ceased to be merely a means to an end and became an end in itself. At its core, racism is a spiritual problem, and it has proven to be a stubborn, difficult foe.

This spiritual problem, which some have called America's "original sin," has provided *the* distinguishing feature between black abolitionism and white abolitionism. White abolitionists wanted to see the end of slavery. Some, however, despite their abolitionist activities, were unable to accord blacks the same level of human dignity that they believed whites possessed. Hence, the defense, rescue, and restoration of the human dignity of blacks would become the defining feature of the African American understanding of what abolitionism really meant.

But what do we mean by human dignity? The question of human dignity has received considerable attention in the social sciences, particularly as more attention has been given to the concept of universal human rights. As political scientists Robert P. Kraynak and Glenn Tinder demonstrate, the concept of human dignity has changed over the centuries, and there is no consensus among contemporary writers. To attempt to craft a fully viable concept of human dignity is beyond the scope of this book. However, I can outline features of human dignity that coincide with what black abolitionists sought to convey as they spoke about their experience of slavery and articulated their understanding of the nature of the abolitionist project. Key elements drawn from the writings of Kraynak, Timothy P. Jackson, Francis Fukuyama, and Raimond Gaita provide important features that contribute to this sketch of the concept of human dignity.[1]

First, human dignity is related to the notion that human beings are created in the image of God *(imago Dei)*. The concept of the *imago Dei* is derived from the Judeo-Christian tradition. Historically, the image of God has been conceived in a number of ways, even though the biblical tradition has not defined the precise way in which humans image God.[2] Whatever way one might choose to understand the *imago Dei*, it is viewed as a quality that God confers in the act of creating the human being; it is a gift, not something one earns. Second, the *imago Dei* is universal, not restricted to certain groups or denied to others. The *imago Dei* is not denied to someone based upon gender, economic class, race, low intelligence, or the presence of disabilities or defects. The donative dimension of this image renders *all* human beings valuable and worthy of respect. Some writers speak of the infinite value of the human person; however, I prefer to say that the value is incalculable.[3] Third, the violation of this dignity distorts the human spirit and deforms the personality. The fourth element is the capacity for an inner life of depth and complexity. This includes the capability to express the full range of human emotions, the capacity for reflection, the capacity to relate to others, to experience joy, and to suffer.[4]

These are all important elements of the concept of human dignity. However, there is another factor that is particularly pertinent as one examines the writings of black abolitionists. There is something about the possession of this dignity that demands to be recognized. As moral philosopher Raimond Gaita eloquently articulates and, I believe, expresses the sentiment of black abolitionists, the need for such acknowledgment is part and parcel of the quest for social justice: "Treat me as a human being, fully as your equal, without condescension."[5] As Gaita notes, this is a plea for justice; however, it is not simply justice understood as equal access to goods and opportunities, but rather justice conceived as equality of respect.[6] The deliberate, systematic denial of that need for equality of respect exacerbates the experience of material deprivations. As Gaita writes, "Those who are the victims of injustice suffer not merely certain determinate forms of natural harm—physical or psychological damage, for example—but also the *injustice of their infliction,* which is a distinct and irreducible source of torment to them."[7] I believe that the writings of black abolitionists support the validity of Gaita's thesis.

For black abolitionists the quest for human dignity involved, of course, equal access to the goods and opportunities theoretically available to all citizens of the United States, as expressed in the Constitution. It also involved the desire to assume the responsibilities that come with equal rights and the desire to participate in the building up of this nation in a way that would enhance the common good. However, this underlying vision of justice assumed requisite equality of respect that would entail blacks' inclusion in a constituency within which claims for equity of access to goods and opportunity could be appropriately pressed.[8] They believed that state and civic institutions as well as the church should, to the degree that is humanly possible, reveal rather than obscure the full humanity of all.[9] In seeking justice in America, black abolitionists sought equality of respect. They wanted recognition that they were part of a common humanity.

It must be emphasized, however, that this quest is *not* to be understood as an assertion that having whites recognize and treat them as human beings would *make* blacks human.[10] Rather, one must regard the quest as a reflection of the *human* need for *acknowledgment* of one's humanity from others. For black abolitionists this human need was made manifest in a number of ways: their sense of outrage; their passionate protest revealed in their narratives and other writings; their willingness to struggle even under the threat of death; and the way black writers sought to illustrate through their evocative descriptions of black life under the yoke of slavery and racism that they were capable of feeling and of suffering deeply, as *any* human being would respond to such injustice.

In addition to this issue of viewing black abolitionism as the quest for the restoration of human dignity, there is another important conclusion one can draw with regard to what distinguishes black abolitionism from white abolitionism. This distinction can be traced to the difference in degree to which white abolitionists, as a whole, were unable to subscribe without reservations to the notion that blacks should be accorded the same respect given to whites.

There has been a tendency in historical studies of the abolitionist movement to focus on the contributions of whites, as if the work of emancipation was something of which blacks were only passive recipients rather than something for which blacks also fought. Though the contribution of whites to abolitionism cannot be underestimated in terms of its impact on the eventual end to slavery, it is important to devote attention to the efforts of blacks and their relationship to the wider abolitionist movement—how and why blacks became involved, the nature of their involvement, and the role that racism and paternalism played in the formation of separate antislavery societies.

To assert that the black abolitionist movement was distinct from and parallel with the larger white abolitionist movement does not belie the fact that black abolitionists were generally willing to participate in interracial antislavery societies. They participated in those societies because they believed that such organizations could best model their vision of the kind of fraternal solidarity among the races that blacks hoped for within society at large. Nevertheless, blacks also organized separate antislavery societies, partly in response to the racism they found within the white abolitionist movement, and partly out of the conviction that they, as fellow blacks, were in a better position to ascertain and meet the needs of their own people. Separate black organizations allowed blacks to formulate their own strategies and implement their own remedies within the back community. These separate societies also allowed blacks to debate and address issues affecting the black community that did not receive adequate attention from white abolitionists. Moreover, further exploration of the black convention movement, and its aims, is also warranted to provide a more comprehensive picture of the abolitionist movement in the United States. In terms of this study, the focus for determining the degree to which the black abolitionist movement was distinct from and parallel to its white counterpart rests with the paternalism and racism that contributed to the inability of whites to affirm fully the vision blacks had of social justice in America.

This book is divided into three parts. Part I, the first three chapters, describes North American slavery and the beginnings of abolitionism in America. Part II, which comprises Chapters 4 through 8, examines the lives and key texts of four black abolitionists; taken together, these lives and texts provide a portrait of black abolitionism as a quest for human dignity. Although they are less renowned than Frederick Douglass, Harriet Tubman, or Sojourner Truth, I selected David Walker, James W. C. Pennington, Henry Highland Garnet, and Samuel Ringgold Ward as representatives of black abolitionism for two reasons. These four left extant writings that passionately and, at times, poignantly articulated the degree to which slavery in North America was especially degrading to the dignity of African Americans. But they also provide a potent witness to the power of the Christian gospel to fuel their commitment to the restoration of the dignity of blacks in American society. Part III, the three remaining chapters, identifies the major obstacle not only to emancipation but to the black quest for recognition of human rights.

There has been some differentiation between the terms *abolitionism* and *antislavery* among scholars, raising the question of whether one term might be more appropriate than the other when talking about the span of the abolitionist movement from the pre-Revolutionary era until the post–Civil War era. Historian Benjamin Quarles has noted that the moderate reformers of the pre-1830s appropriated the "strong" word "abolitionism" in their societies. However, because of their more moderate stance toward ending slavery, their radical successors were forced to adopt the "milder" designation "antislavery" in their organizational names.[11] Historian Dwight Lowell Dumond supports this differentiation when he contends that there was a "vast difference" between antislavery and abolitionism, and that to say that someone was opposed to slavery was not to say very much other than that such a person was not a devotee of the argument that slavery was a positive good.[12] Dumond identifies several criteria that marked a true abolitionist: (1) willingness by those who owned no slaves to bring about a state of emancipation by compulsion;

(2) refusal to countenance expatriation; and (3) insistence upon according to the emancipated slaves all the privileges and civil liberties of free citizens.[13] Dumond's point is that an abolitionist was opposed to slavery but also actively engaged not only in bringing about the end of the practice but also in ensuring that the emancipated received all the rights and privileges accorded any free citizen of the United States. While there is a great deal of appeal to the distinctions Dumond and Quarles make between the two terms, a strong case also can be made that strict adherence to the distinction would eliminate a good number of activists in the movement from the 1830s onward, despite the distinctively more militant agitation that differentiates pre-1830s abolitionist activity from that of the post-1830s. This is because racial prejudice precluded full support for all three of Dumond's criteria. Therefore, in the interest of simplicity, I have chosen to use the terms *abolitionism* and *antislavery* interchangeably.

I also use the terms *racism, white racism,* and *white supremacy* interchangeably, although *white supremacy* is often employed today to designate fringe groups that espouse a militant form of racial hatred. I use the term *white supremacy* despite this because I believe that it truly captures the essence of what lies behind racial domination in the way that the terms *white racism* or simply *racism* often do not. White supremacy is not confined to the individual or personal dimension, dealing with likes and dislikes based upon personal preferences alone, but constitutes a *system* of domination that is furnished with social, political, economic, and philosophical structures of control. White supremacy is not confined to the cowards who hide behind hooded robes or to those who have shaved their heads, covered their bodies with tattoos, and tote an arsenal of weaponry. It is a system that envelopes the well-meaning liberal and ultraconservative, sometimes unwittingly, because it shapes the entire cultural apparatus and the world view of the dominant group that lives in it. It is the kind of ideology that casts its tentacles far and wide, even upon ordinary, "respectable," good people.

Although the term *African American* is presently used to refer to people of African descent in the United States, I have chosen to give primacy to the term *black* instead. During the time period covered in this text, mainly 1619 to 1865, black people were not legally American citizens. A major reason for this was because of their race (and color). Therefore, it seems more appropriate to use the term *black* in this context, in keeping with the deepest, longing reflection in the quest of black abolitionists: to privilege their personhood *as blacks.*

On occasion I use the term *America* to refer exclusively to the United States. Although I recognize the validity of the objection of those who criticize the U.S. appropriation of that term (which can refer to Latin or South America or Canada), I have elected to follow convention in this instance.

PART I

SLAVERY AND ABOLITIONISM IN AMERICA

Chapter 1

North American Slavery

An Assault on Human Dignity

"To write the history of the conflict which resulted in the Civil War, one must recount the nature of slavery: a 'social malady' that was so deep-seated that it often threatened the principles of civil rights associated with the nation's birth."[1] With that observation, historian Dwight Lowell Dumond proceeds to paint a grim portrait of the impact of slavery on the United States. The controversy over this "social malady" sundered churches and political parties; adversely affected the family as an institution, and severed the nation. His characterization is certainly accurate in terms of the impact that slavery had upon the sociopolitical dimensions of life in the United States. However, our contention here is that slavery was not only a deep-seated "social malady" but also a grave *theological* one whose impact on the black community and adverse effect on relations between blacks and whites have yet to be redeemed.

Before we can assess black abolitionism as a quest for human dignity, we must determine the nature of slavery in North America, whether it differed substantially from the practice of slavery in other contexts, and whether there was anything about the practice of slavery in North America that would lead black resisters to believe that the dignity of black people under the system was inherently in jeopardy. Although a thorough examination of slavery worldwide is beyond the scope of this study, a relatively brief survey of slavery within various historical contexts can provide a measure of comparison that enables us to draw conclusions about slavery in America and its impact upon its black victims. Further, such a survey can enable us to understand why the restoration of black dignity became a central theme in black abolitionism. The work of Milton Meltzer, David Brion Davis, Don E. Fehrenbacher, Stanley M. Elkins, Dwight Lowell Dumond, Gerald Sorin, Leon F. Litwack, Arthur Zilversmit, Louis Filler, and John Hope Franklin can help to establish the historical context of slavery in North America.

HUMAN BONDAGE IN THE ANCIENT WORLD

The existence of slavery is nearly as old as the existence of human life. In his study of the history of slavery worldwide, historian Milton Meltzer notes that slavery was known to have existed among the Sumerian peoples over three thousand years before the beginning of the Christian era. Most of the slaves in the southern half of the Mesopotamian plain, which the Sumerians occupied, had been captured during frequent wars with neighboring city-states. However, they could be ransomed and returned to freedom at any time. The Sumerians were succeeded in political power by western Semites or Amorites around 2000 BCE, who founded new kingdoms in Mesopotamia. By 1800 BCE one of those kingdoms was governed by King Hammurabi, who conquered the competing kingdoms and united diverse ethnic groups under a single government in Mesopotamia. Hammurabi made social and administrative reforms and established a justice system of common law referred to as codes. The Code of Law encouraged slavery but also recognized that slaves were valuable to society and required protection from their owners.

Slavery in Mesopotamia steadily increased. Assyrian and Babylonian slaves were permitted a great deal of independence. Meltzer notes that although their status rendered them no more than property, and they were considered devoid of will or personality, they were allowed to own livestock, real estate, and other property, including other slaves. The slaves were permitted to participate in various important aspects of social life like any citizen, including engaging in trading and banking and conducting business. Some even attained high administrative positions.

The Egyptians, who lived in the valley of the Nile River, about one thousand miles west of Mesopotamia, lived in relative security from invasions, and this contributed to their different way of life; this difference influenced their use of slaves. The bottom rung of society consisted of the peasants, who were technically free, but, like serfs, were bound to the soil and the property of anyone who bought the land that they occupied. The peasant population was large, and peasants provided the basic labor; thus, the number of slaves (primarily prisoners of war) was not large. The Hebrews, who entered Egypt around 1700 BCE to seek refuge in the Nile delta from drought or famine in Palestine, settled on the eastern edge of the Nile delta, where they multiplied and prospered. Within 150 years the Egyptians enslaved the Hebrews. The Hebrews were subsequently delivered from slavery and, in turn, conquered Canaan.

Although the Hebrews were enjoined from participating in slavery by tenets of their faith, they, like other peoples of that time, practiced slavery. Their slaves included those who were burdened by debt or who had sold themselves or their children into slavery to avoid starvation. Meltzer indicates that slavery became widespread during this time and continued into the beginning of the Christian era. As such, the institution became so deeply woven into the economic and social fabric of the ancient world that Hebrew lawmakers sought to lighten the burden of slavery when they found the institution too difficult to eradicate. Slavery for debt in Hebrew society was not considered permanent, and provisions were made to allow for release from debt in the year of Jubilee, which came every fifty years.

When the Greeks established colonies along the Mediterranean and Black Sea shorelines between 800 and 600 BCE, they increasingly employed slaves to produce a surplus of goods for sale as the expansion of the economy continued. This led to a gradual transformation of domestic slavery into industrial slavery. Some Greek slaves were hired out, living apart from their masters. These contracted slaves enjoyed a degree of independence that included freedom to form their own families. Meltzer asserts that human bondage was a universal custom, and it was taken for granted. The slavery practiced in ancient Greece was not based on race, color, or caste. Most slaves were foreigners (non-Greeks) acquired through warfare, piracy, kidnapping, or shipwrecks. The Greeks saw no contradiction between the ideal of democracy and the practice of a slavocracy, because citizenship (which was denied to women) was hereditary and thus inaccessible to foreigners. Full citizenship was limited to a privileged few.

Rome superseded classical Greece as a major world power. By 272 BCE, Rome had conquered Greek cities and had added them to its confederation. By 114 BCE, Rome owned or ruled nearly every land on the margins of the Mediterranean. It was during these years of conquest that slavery became a powerful force in Roman life. But much earlier, by the fourth century BCE, the basic pattern of Western slavery was formed. The capture and sale of prisoners of war was the chief source of slavery for the last three hundred years of the Roman Republic. Slaves in Rome (and in the ancient world in general) were allowed certain legal capacities and were afforded at least theoretical protection against murder and severe bodily harm. Because of this, Roman jurists openly acknowledged that the slave was both a person and a thing.[2] Historian David Brion Davis contends that none of the ancient societies rendered the distinction between the slave and the free person as sharply as the distinction drawn in America.[3] Meltzer observes that while Rome became the greatest empire of the ancient world, maintaining power for six hundred years, the empire fell in the fifth century CE, and one of the causes was the prevalence of slavery.

THE ATLANTIC SLAVE TRADE

The European slave trade began in 1441 with Portuguese ships raiding the Atlantic coast of Africa. Portugal led the expansion of Europe over the seas in the fifteenth century, with Spain close behind. David Brion Davis maintains that Spain and Portugal were the transitional link between slavery as it had existed throughout history and as it was to develop in the Americas.[4] In 1492 Christopher Columbus reached the New World and subsequently instituted a colonization process built upon slave labor. The white settlers to the Caribbean islands sought labor for the sugar, tobacco, and cotton plantations, which required large-scale production and cheap labor in order to be profitable. Initially, the settlers used the indigenous population; however, these peoples died quickly due to the heavy labor and the diseases that the white settlers transmitted to them. When the indigenous peoples proved unsuitable, the settlers used European indentured servants and convicts. Eventually, though, the settlers imported African slaves, who could be obtained from the western coast of Africa.

Domestic slavery among African peoples had existed for quite some time. However, the slavery practiced among African societies did not include legal extinction of human rights or the denial of human personality. Although the African slaves were of lesser status than free people, they had certain rights and their owners had certain duties toward them. Also, a certain degree of fluidity in African society made it possible for a captive to advance from vassal to free person and even to chief. Slavery within African society did not mean permanent imprisonment in servitude with little or no hope of liberation. Meltzer indicates that the experience of slavery within the European slave system vastly differed from that which had been known among African societies. Kidnapping, piracy, treachery, and brutality marked the Atlantic slave trade. Meltzer maintains that the pressure to obtain the maximum profit out of the trade was so intense that traders sometimes defeated their own purpose by destroying their human commodity.[5]

The flourishing of slavery in regions of the United States was directly related to its economic profitability. Prior to America's War of Independence there were no sectional boundaries to black slavery. Historian Leon F. Litwack notes that every colony recognized it and sharply defined the legal position of free and enslaved blacks.[6] Although the slave population of the North was relatively small, black slavery was a common and accepted practice there as well as in the South.[7] In general, northern masters owned only a few blacks, but there were areas in the North where the plantation system was reproduced on a small scale.[8] Historian Arthur Zilversmit observes that the practice of slavery was more prominent in the middle colonies. Owning slaves was a widespread, common, and accepted practice in colonial New

York.[9] The pattern of slave-holding in New Jersey and Pennsylvania was much the same as in New York: there were many masters who relied on a few blacks, but large holdings were common in some areas.[10] Eventually, in the midst of revolutionary and anti-colonial consensus against Britain, Northern antislavery sentiment grew to such an extent that New England colonies and (post–1776) states gradually abolished black chattel.[11] However, proslavery sentiment in the North persisted long after the Constitutional Convention and the formal abolition of Northern slavery.[12] Although New England initially led the way in terms of the slave trade, eventually it became more profitable to sell slaves to the plantation colonies.[13] So, as historian Louis Filler maintains, overall the North was more significant for its role in the transportation of slaves than for its furtherance of slavery institutions.[14] Nevertheless, he notes, the North and South were so intricately related, commercially and socially, as far as black slaves were concerned, that it is a major problem to determine precisely what drew North and South apart over the issue of slavery.[15]

Although slavery in the North faded because there was no strong demand for slave labor, the slave trade was important for the production of tobacco, rice, and indigo, which were the staples of the economy of the lower South. The economic system of the South relied on slave labor, and slaves were viewed as much as articles of commerce as were the crops they produced. Black slavery played a major role in the early development of the Americas and in the growth of commercial capitalism.[16] But American slavery was more than an economic institution. It represented the ultimate limit of dehumanization, of treating and regarding black people as things.[17] Further, two salient features of North American slavery that had not been widespread in ancient slavery were the racial basis of enslavement and the legal impediments to manumission.[18]

FEATURES OF SLAVERY IN THE UNITED STATES

Davis makes three important points about the distinction between the concept of slavery and the reality of it. First, the ancient ideal of personal subordination was modified by Christianity but continued to influence medieval and early modern thought, even in those places where chattel bondage had disappeared. Second, to the degree that actual forms of servitude approximated the concept of slavery found, for example, in Roman law, those forms treated people as objects to be manipulated, humiliated, and exploited. Finally, the contradictions inherent in slavery were not confined to theory alone but invariably were manifested in historical circumstances.[19] As Davis points out, although the ideal slave was a model of ideal submission, no one could forget that inanimate objects such as tools and instruments could not run away or rebel or otherwise respond negatively to forced bondage. Thus, societies could not escape the reality that the slave was a conscious being and that attempts to bend the will of the slave to that of the master invariably led to conflict. Because of this inherent conflict, societies have usually experienced a sense of uneasiness with slavery. This was no different when slavery spread to the New World.

Davis argues that by the 1760s, when slavery was taking hold in North America, there was nothing unprecedented about chattel slavery, even the slavery of one ethnic group to another.[20] Nor were the central characteristics of slavery in America unique.[21] The three defining characteristics of slavery were that (1) the slave was the property of another person, (2) the slave's will was subject to his or her owner's authority, and (3) the slave's labor was obtained through coercion.[22] Although there were atrocities in the ancient practice of slavery that rivaled those in the nineteenth century, the slave system in the southern states of America (as well as in the West Indies) was quite different in that the free population in the Americas was separated from the slaves by racial and cultural differences. For the most part, slaves were deprived of the hope of manumission, and their lives were regimented in a highly organized system that was geared toward maximum production for a market economy.[23] For Davis, the most disturbing aspect of American slavery was the slaves' lack of protection from murder and physical assault.[24]

As we continue to examine the development of slavery in North America, we see the emergence of an American caste system with the corresponding rational justification for it appearing somewhat later. When the first blacks came to British North America in 1619, they were brought ashore on a Dutch ship, illustrating the international origins of the slave system in the United States.[25] Over the next few decades additional blacks in relatively small numbers were brought to Virginia and introduced into the other English colonies. Economist Gunnar Myrdal indicates that blacks in British North America were first treated as indentured servants and then, beginning in the middle of the seventeenth century, "were pushed down into chattel slavery while the white servants were allowed to work off their bond."[26] Historically, because of inadequate and inconsistent record-keeping, there is some controversy regarding the status of these blacks. Their status was not uniform, for some were held in bondage only for a period of years and then received their freedom, just as white apprentices and indentured servants were. Nevertheless, we do know that perpetual and hereditary servitude soon became the rule, and by the 1660s it was being formalized in colonial laws.[27]

Historian Don E. Fehrenbacher indicates that this momentous change was justified for a time in terms of culture and biblical authority, namely, that "the Negro was a heathen and a barbarian, an outcast among the people of the earth, a descendant of Noah's son Ham, cursed by God himself and doomed to be a servant forever on account of an ancient sin."[28] It was not until later that the defense of slavery became biological in character as well. One might say that first came blacks, then the institution of slavery, and finally racism of the kind that asserts the genetic inferiority of blacks.[29]

THE IMPACT OF RACISM

Fehrenbacher and other scholars indicate that a fully articulated theory of biological (and therefore permanent) black inferiority did not emerge until the second quarter of the nineteenth century. This theory developed in close association with the Southern defense of slavery as a "positive good" and in response to the intensified abolitionist crusade after the 1830s.[30] Racism in its ultimate, intellectualized form became a conspicuous part of the U.S. rationale for slavery only after nearly two centuries of slavery's existence as an institution, and slavery itself became institutionalized and legalized only several decades after the presence of blacks in the English colonies.

Fehrenbacher maintains that this "double time-lag" seems to indicate a slow evolution of race prejudice as a concomitant, or perhaps even as an outgrowth, of the slave system. But he also notes that whenever enslavement began, it was imposed selectively on a racial basis. He raises the question of whether this indicates that there was present, to facilitate the degradation of blacks into chattel slavery, pressure of strong preconceptions and elemental feelings amounting to rudiments of the full-blown racial doctrine perfected in the nineteenth century. He concedes that slavery and race prejudice were no doubt perpetuated and mutually strengthened by the continuing resonance between them. However, in order to determine the origins of each, one has to look past the formalities of enacted law and elaborated theory into the "dimmer realm of private, seldom-expressed attitudes, random thoughts, and unrationalized behavior."[31]

I suggest that this realm was not so dim. The fact that when enslavement was imposed it was done selectively on the basis of race strongly indicates the presence of racial bias. The fact that a fully rationalized doctrine emerged later does not belie the presence of its existence prior to that formal articulation. What Fehrenbacher goes on to say lends even further credence to this supposition.

In discussing the difference between black servitude and white servitude, Fehrenbacher notes that white servitude was also involuntary, incurred as punishment for crime or sometimes as the result of kidnapping carried on outside the law.[32] But it was only in the case of Africans that captivity was the normal and universal prelude to servitude. He states that purchasers of blacks during the early colonial period were "merely" new receivers in a traffic that already had a long history. To Fehrenbacher, their willingness to buy indicates that they had been conditioned to accept the fundamental assumption of the slave trade: "Africans, by their nature, were fair game for capture and uniquely fitted for servitude."[33]

Fehrenbacher maintains that colonial servitude, black and white, took root in response to the practical need for cheap, controllable labor, especially on Southern plantations. However, the economic explanation of slavery, which would become increasingly valid with the growth of the institution, does not fully explain its origins. At least two factors support his conclusion. First, at an early date slavery penetrated New England, where no strong need for it existed.[34] Second, even in the Southern colonies slavery acquired firm legal status well before blacks replaced white servants as the principal labor force. Thus, the installation of slavery appears to have preceded the rise of a pressing economic need for it. The institution was not born of necessity but was instead a "mere convenience" at the time of its introduction into England's mainland colonies.[35] Uniform legal rules for slavery began in 1660.

According to Fehrenbacher, the swiftness with which black servitude was made "not only lifelong but hereditary indicates deep-rooted assumptions essentially biological in character." Reference to scriptural authority and emphasis on the contrast between Christian civilization and heathen savagery had been the earlier prominent justifications of slavery.[36] Before the first blacks landed in Virginia, however, the association of Africans with slavery and the assumption of black inferiority had become firmly set and intertwined.[37]

By the eve of the American Revolution slavery was not only legally established in all thirteen colonies but so firmly implanted in the Southern colonies that blacks constituted about 40 percent of their population.[38] Further, in all the colonies African slavery was lifelong and hereditary, with a child of mixed free and slave parentage assuming at birth the status of its mother. By law a slave was reduced "in considerable degree from a person to a thing, having no legitimate will of its own and belonging bodily to its owner."[39] Like property, a slave could be bought and sold. "As animate property, he could be compelled to work, and his offspring belonged absolutely to the master."[40] Fehrenbacher goes on to say that "a slave was in some respects like a domestic animal, being an item of wealth, virtually a beast of burden, and a creature requiring constant supervision and restraint."[41]

Fehrenbacher notes that, aside from the Quakers, slavery remained a largely "unexamined fact of life" prior to the mid-eighteenth century. However, in the 1760s there were new currents of liberal thought from the European Enlightenment (which contributed much to the ideology of the American Revolution). This thought, in turn, encouraged "uneasy reflection" on the rationale of slavery.[42] The rhetoric of the colonial struggle with England soon heightened the contradiction of freedom and servitude in America.[43] This was particularly true in the North. Fehrenbacher observes that many were troubled that the language of colonial resistance to England could be read as an indictment of slaveholding.

According to historian Stanley M. Elkins, as that contradiction became more disconcerting, a common tale appeared in both the North and the South concerning the way they had dealt with questions of slavery thirty years before the Civil War. Each side expressed itself with a "simple moral severity," viewing slavery as though it were a "gross fact" with certain "universal, immutable, abstract features" that were not affected by considerations of time and place.[44] For the Northern reformer, "every other concrete fact concerning slavery was dwarfed by its character as a moral evil."[45] The Southerner replied that slavery was a positive moral good, a social arrangement sanctioned in scripture (and thus by God).[46] Thus, it was believed that an inferior race must live under the domination of a superior. Neither side seemed capable of viewing slavery as a social institution, functioning by laws and logic like other institutions, or seeing that it was changeable, fashioned after human custom and capable of infinite variation from one culture to another.[47]

Beyond that, Elkins contends that there was nothing "natural" about black slavery. It had no necessary tie with either tropical climate or tropical crops. The institution first appeared in Virginia and Maryland, where the climate was not tropical. The staple crop, tobacco, could be grown as far north as Canada. There were no characteristics that made blacks peculiarly suited either to slavery or to the labor of tobacco culture.[48] Slavery had not been limited to a particular race in the past, and the earliest planters of colonial Virginia appear to have preferred a white work force from England, Scotland, and Ireland rather than blacks from Africa.[49] Agreeing with other scholars Elkins maintains that slavery, considered as servile bondage, had existed in other places for centuries, even in Africa. Yet nothing was inherent, even in the fact of black slavery, that should have made it necessary for slavery to take the form that it did in America.

Elkins argues that even though the first shipload of twenty blacks arrived in Virginia in 1619, it was not until the 1660s that the key issue with regard to a definition of their status—namely, their term of servitude—was clearly fixed in law.[50] By the 1660s halting of manumission and impediments to movement into society as artisans and property ownership emerged through the imposition of laws.

NORTH AMERICAN SLAVERY: A CLOSED SYSTEM

In Latin America the tension and balance among the church, the crown, and plantation agriculture prevented slavery from being carried by the planting class to its ultimate conclusion.[51] Slavery in that context allowed for the development of men and women as moral beings because it was an open system. Also, "the rights of personality implicit in the ancient traditions of slavery and in the church's most venerable assumptions on the nature of the human soul were . . . in a vital sense conserved."[52] However, this was not the case in North America. The kind of checks that had been found in Latin America were absent. Elkins maintains that the legal structure that supported slavery in the Northern hemisphere had been shaped by the demands of staple-raising capitalism and had defined slaves as chattel, leaving their character as moral individuals in legal obscurity. In this sense we can speak of slavery in North America as a closed system.

Dwight Lowell Dumond describes the predicament of the black slave in this closed system. Slaves were robbed of their inalienable rights as human beings. They were denied ownership of their bodies. They had no freedom of choice about the use of their time or the kinds of occupations they held. They were denied the rights of marriage, family life, and paternal authority. They were not free to worship according to their conscience. They were denied the right to cultivate their minds, to use their unique talents, and to influence their fellow men and women. They could not protect themselves, their homes, or their families against violence. They had no protection under the law. Slaves were denied the most elementary human rights.[53]

But, Dumond rightly contends, slavery as an economic system was of small account compared with slavery as a system of racial adjustment and social control. Belief in the biological inequality and the racial inferiority of blacks not only sustained slavery and colonization, but it also determined the attitude of the public, the zeal of law-enforcement officials, the reasoning of judicial bodies, the efficiency of administrative functionaries, and the definition of policies by legislatures and Congress in all matters pertaining to blacks and abolition.[54]

Historian Gerald Sorin adds to the contour of slavery in North America. He notes that throughout Western history slavery had been viewed by many as the ultimate dehumanization. He states that the New World was represented as the "promised land" where humankind could make a fresh start. Further, America, in particular, represented a land in which there were no vestiges of former tyrannies. It was envisioned as a place where all people could undergo a rebirth and a fulfillment of human aspirations. American slavery brought a profound contradiction to that vision and created a source of extraordinary psychic unease.[55] Thus, elaborate justifications were required to make slavery seem more compatible with American's vision of itself.

An important assumption undergirding slavery, according to Sorin, was that some people *by nature* were incapable of maintaining or governing themselves. When white men first made contact with blacks in Africa, they were already preconditioned culturally to see blackness as something negative or inferior.[56] In order to defend slavery, they needed to see blacks as substandard. African differences were exaggerated and, despite evidence to the contrary, were taken as proof of racial inferiority. Blacks were viewed as the product of a separate creation, bearing in their color the mark of ancient sins, and they were punished with the need for subordination to higher authority. Yet, Sorin maintains, despite these rationalizations slavery continued to be a source of discomfort. People found it difficult to escape altogether the feeling that slavery was incompatible with the progress of the scientific enlightenment, the new directions of Christianity, and the developing idea of natural rights.

Sorin contends that racism was the great limiting factor for abolitionist growth, that it knew no sectional or ideological boundaries. Belief in the inferiority of blacks pervaded the consciousness of white America, North and South; abolitionists did not always escape this belief either. Slavery made the idea of black inferiority more entrenched, and as whites enjoyed more social and economic advantages, the notion of black inferiority became even harder to surrender. He writes, "Faced with the continued existence of an 'evil' institution in a 'good' society, defenders of slavery articulated and internalized a more thoroughly racist rationale for the institution."[57]

Given the distinctions that have been drawn between North American slavery and slavery in other socio-historical contexts, and given the ideological and philosophical foundations that supported American slavery, it is useful to consider those issues in light of their impact upon slavery as it was practiced in the South and some regions of the North.

As black historian John Hope Franklin indicates, Southerners excluded blacks from their religious and moral conceptions of freedom, even evolving the new notion that the enslavement of blacks was essential to the white man's freedom.[58] Slave Codes were adopted to strictly regulate the activity of slaves. In most cases, he notes, slaves were not persons but property, and the laws were designed to protect the ownership of such property and to protect whites against any dangers that might arise from the presence of large numbers of blacks. The Slave Codes were designed to maintain slaves in a position of due subordination in order that optimum discipline and work production could be achieved.

Furthermore, slaves had no standing in the courts: they could not be a party to a suit, they could not offer testimony except against another slave or a free black, and they could not make contracts. Slaves could not own property generally. They could not strike a white person, even in self-defense. Yet, the killing of a slave, however malicious the act, was rarely regarded as murder. The rape of female slaves was regarded as a crime, but only because it involved "trespassing."[59]

As a way of justifying the system, slave owners nearly always sought to convey the impression that the slaves were docile, tractable, and happy; thus they defended the institution as "benign."[60] The plantation bred indecency in human relations. Slaves were immediate victims of the barbarity of the system that exploited the sex of the women and the work of everyone. Moreover, Franklin maintains, the psychological situation created by the master-slave relationship stimulated terrorism and brutality.[61]

NORTH AMERICAN SLAVERY: SOME CONCLUSIONS

At the beginning of the chapter I sought to determine the nature of slavery in North America. I asked specifically whether slavery in North America differed substantially from slavery in other contexts, and to what degree its practice inherently threatened the dignity of African American slaves. This brief historical survey of slavery yields several conclusions. First, the practice of slavery in North America shared a number of features with the practice in other societies: the slave was viewed as property, the slave's will was subject to that of his or her owner, and the slave's labor was coerced. Second, there were several distinctive elements in the practice of slavery in the United States: its permanent, hereditary character; its racialization; the insistence on the inherent inferiority of blacks and the concomitant belief that blacks were inherently suited for slavery; and the elaborate rationalizations to justify slavery in the face of the double contradiction that slavery heightened in a society that ostensibly held to Christian principles and idealized the notion of liberty. Third, the particular constellation of distinctive features of North American slavery inherently threatened the dignity of black slaves. The permanent, hereditary character of North American slavery left little chance for manumission and ensured that future generations would be doomed to a life of servitude. Within a relatively short period of time the practice of slavery became reserved largely for blacks, who were viewed as inferior beings designed for servitude. Such a dehumanizing system inherently threatened the dignity of black slaves. Black abolitionists certainly viewed the system in that way. They found the practice of slavery in the United States especially egregious because this dehumanizing system occurred in a nation that claimed to be Christian and espoused the ideology of political freedom.

North Americans did not invent slavery. However, their singling out peoples of African descent for permanent, hereditary, chattel slavery, in which blacks were denied protection under the law, made slavery a "peculiar" institution indeed. As some in the nation wrestled with their uneasy consciences, a movement emerged that would bring pressure to bear upon the institution of slavery and culminate in civil war: abolitionism. Because of chattel slavery and the legal and customary practices that presided over the degradation of blacks, systematic *de*humanization was the biggest burden of the system that black abolitionists, in particular, sought to overthrow.

Chapter 2

Seasons of Abolitionism

Abolitionism in Context

We have previously noted that a number of people felt discomfort over slavery, regardless of their attitude toward people of African descent. The philosophical rhetoric that fueled the French and American Revolutions, with its assertions regarding the natural rights of man, and the theological impulses fed by the Great Awakening made the consciences of whites uneasy and opened the door to abolitionist thinking. But the path of abolitionism was not linear. Pre-Revolutionary abolitionist activity tended to be reduced to moral suasion, a concern for the rights of slave holders, and a certain optimism that slavery would die out on its own in due course. By the early 1800s, with the invention of technology that made slavery even more profitable in the South, the optimism concerning a gradual end of slavery disappeared. In its place emerged a more aggressive approach to abolitionist activity. However, even with the denotation of a gradualism-turned-radicalism, the progression of abolitionism was neither as rapid nor as straightforward as such a division might suggest.

Historians of the abolitionist movement have divided the stages of abolitionist activity in various ways in order to demonstrate that abolitionism was neither static in terms of the pressure brought to bear upon society in order to achieve emancipation nor monolithic in terms of the kinds of people who participated. Some of the staging of the movement focuses primarily on the work of white abolitionists. Other scholars divide the stages based upon the participation of blacks within the wider movement. Still others focus upon the activity of abolitionists in the nineteenth century only, perhaps because the most significant amount of activity occurred in that century. These demarcations and classifications have been designed to express the complexity and variation within the movement.

Historian Gerald Sorin notes two camps within abolitionism. There were some Americans prior to the Civil War who felt antipathy toward the institution of slavery. Many of these people were explicitly opposed to the institution when it appeared that slavery was having a detrimental effect on the quality of American society in general. Sorin argues that the motivation behind their opposition was driven by several things. First, some opponents of slavery were concerned about its impact upon America's economic growth. Second, they felt that the South's reaction to the criticism of slavery threatened to undermine white civil liberties. Third, they believed that slavery and the slavocracy resulting from it stood opposed to the values of a growing bourgeois democracy. Other opponents of slavery, at least until the Civil War, were satisfied to advocate containment of the institution within its existing boundaries. Sorin indicates that even when those whites came to see the injustice of slavery itself and came to favor emancipation, many remained uninterested in, and even violently opposed to, racial integration.[1]

Sorin, like other scholars, including Benjamin Quarles, maintains that it is difficult to provide an exclusive profile of the men and women who participated in the abolitionist movement. Exposure to the values of religious benevolence and evangelism was a motivator, but there were many other Americans who were also exposed to those values who did not become abolitionists or even opposed abolitionism. Therefore, Sorin concludes, a religious explanation alone is inadequate to explain the impulse.[2]

Dwight Lowell Dumond differentiates the variety within the movement by identifying three periods in the history of the antislavery. The first period centers on the activities of the American Colonization Society, which was founded in 1816 to repatriate free blacks to Africa. This organization drew its support from all sections of the country and from all classes: slave holders and those who did not own slaves, proslavery and antislavery advocates. This first period ended with the organization of the American Anti-Slavery Society, which was founded in 1833 to promote abolitionism. The period between July 1832 and September 1834 was a "preparatory period" for the complete acceptance of abolitionist doctrine. This period convinced white abolitionists of several things: First, colonization was impracticable; the motivation for it was race prejudice; and it strengthened rather than weakened the institution of slavery. Second, slave holders would never voluntarily enter upon a program of gradual emancipation. Third, the display of intolerance that greeted the mildest discussion of the subject raised the controversy from the realm of specific reform in a particular section and "presaged another episode in the ageless struggle for human rights."[3] Dumond dates the second period from 1833 to 1839. During this period the lines for and against slavery were sharply drawn. The fundamental principles of anti slavery doctrine were clarified, and the North was "abolitionized" and covered with a vast network of antislavery societies.[4] The third period began with the adoption of the principles of direct political action by some of the abolitionists in 1839 and the organization of the Liberty Party, a political party dedicated to the abolitionist cause.[5]

Dumond reminds us that slavery was a controversial issue even at the time the Constitutional Convention of 1787 was in deliberation. In fact, it threatened to disrupt the Convention, raising doubts as to the ratification of the new instrument of government and calling forth dire prophecies of future discord between sections of the country.[6] Every Northern state had abolished slavery before the closing of the foreign slave trade in 1808,[7] while no Southern state had done so.[8]

Black historian John Hope Franklin divides the abolitionist movement between a nonmilitant, gradualist phase and the militant antislavery phase. Franklin notes, however, that there were people who not only opposed slavery as an institution but developed arguments opposing it long before the emergence of the militant abolitionists movement of the 1830s. A steady increase in antislavery sentiment in the North occurred after 1815 as a result of more ministers, newspaper editors, and other leaders of public opinion condemning the institution as evil. Three specific events between 1829 and 1831 precipitated the more militant form of abolitionism: the publication and dissemination of David

Walker's *Appeal* (1829), which was a powerful black jeremiad about the evils of slavery; the appearance of William Lloyd Garrison's newspaper *Liberator* (1831), which influenced abolitionist activity in the North and led to an increase in the denunciation of antislavery activity, small as it was, in the South; and the unsuccessful revolt of Nat Turner in 1831. During the more militant, post–1830s phase of abolitionism blacks played a larger role.

As previously noted, there are other ways of dating and delineating the various periods of abolitionist activity. For our purposes it is helpful to chronicle the phases of abolitionist activity movement wide in order to be able to identify more readily the theological, sociological, political, and economic influences that gave shape to the movement as a whole. But more important than capturing the facets of the movement is that these divisions help to identify the impact of influences *on blacks* in particular. This attempt to chronicle the movement, as proposed below, assists in clarifying the level of participation of blacks in the wider movement during the eighteenth and nineteenth centuries. It is also helpful to divide the period of antislavery activity into decades, particularly during the nineteenth century, when significant sociopolitical events and legal enactments had a great impact upon the development of the antislavery movement in relation to blacks and culminated in the Civil War.

Gerald Sorin's division of abolitionist "camps" tells us a bit about the nature of involvement of certain abolitionist types but does not deal with the kinds of developments that shaped and refined abolitionist activity. Also, his description of abolitionist camps addresses only white abolitionism, providing no description of nonwhite abolitionist sentiment. Although dividing antislavery activity into a pre-militant or gradualist period and a militant period, as John Hope Franklin does, has some merit in terms of characterizing the nature of abolitionist activity, this division indicates little about what shaped the two periods in significant ways. Dwight Dumond's classification of abolitionist activity attempts to be more refined, noting particular periods by the emergence of significant developments within the abolitionist movement, but his classification does not address abolitionist activity in relation to its impact upon blacks.

I propose a more nuanced division within abolitionist activity that encompasses both white and black abolitionism but also takes into account events within the movement that relate specifically to significant sociopolitical developments that altered the tenor of the movement in distinct ways that had an impact on blacks. The divisions I propose are these:

> The Colonial Period: 1700 to 1800
> The Gradualist Period: 1800 to 1830
> The Militant Period: 1830 to 1840
> The Early Political Period: 1840 to 1850
> The Late Political Period: 1850 to 1860
> The Civil War Period: 1860 to 1865

Of course, there is a certain amount of arbitrariness in the dates assigned to these periods, and there is some degree of overlap concerning the nature of certain abolitionist activity between the periods. However, this proposed delineation helps to identify more accurately the prominent features of specific abolitionist activity and provides a useful way to categorize some abolitionists during the course of the movement. The length between the earlier phases of abolitionism is greater because the movement was in its nascent period of development, when the level of activity was lower and religious and sociopolitical events that would have a positive impact on abolitionism were few. After 1800 there was an increase in such events, hence the shorter periods between categories.

THE COLONIAL PERIOD (1700–1800)

The initial stage of abolitionism coincided with the period of colonial development in America leading up to the revolutionary activity that culminated in the establishment of the United States. The humanitarian philosophy of the eighteenth century, which fueled both the French and the American revolutions, helped to foster antislavery sentiment. Although this sentiment was dampened in the South as it found new opportunities for the profitable use of slaves, and the North concerned itself with its own economic and political problems, the philosophy of the eighteenth century disturbed the consciences of some with regard to whether the institution of slavery could be justified. Naturally, blacks opposed slavery before the American Revolution as a matter of self-interest, long before the development of an organized movement dedicated to the abolition of slavery as an institution. Slaves in Massachusetts were known to bring action against their masters for freedom before the War for Independence. Further, during and after the Revolutionary War, blacks petitioned the state and federal governments to outlaw the slave trade and to embark upon a program of general emancipation.[9]

Another group noted for abolitionist sentiment in this early period was the Quakers, who offered the only significant movement against slavery in colonial America.[10] Quakers reinforced their objections to slavery by emancipating those who had been enslaved within the Quaker community. Emancipation among Quakers occurred in the eighteenth century in New England, New York, Maryland (Baltimore), Virginia, and North Carolina, rapidly following emancipation in Pennsylvania.[11] Of particular note in the Quaker community is John Woolman, who became an important channel through which antislavery sentiment reached the conscience of the Quakers of America. Although the American Revolution placed slavery into the background for a while, Quakers resumed antislavery activity shortly after the war. During the two decades after the establishment of the Federal Union in 1787, the philosophical ideas from the Revolution led to doubts about the ethics of slave-holding, and these ideas began to affect some members of other Christian denominations.[12] Quakers put pressure on Congress at this time, although their initial efforts proved ineffective as a serious threat to slavery. The turn of the eighteenth century marked the climax of the American Quaker effort of abolitionism, which had begun in 1688. After 1800 the antislavery stance of Quakers was reduced to "quiet testimony."[13]

THE GRADUALIST PERIOD (1800–1830)

The gradualist period encompasses the post-Revolutionary phase of the American republic. One development of this period was the birth of the American Colonization Society (ACS) in 1816. The Rev. Robert Finley, a Presbyterian minister from New Jersey, had been searching for a way to help blacks, particularly free ones. The assumption of Finley, and others as well, was that free blacks and whites could not live together harmoniously; therefore, voluntary emigration of "the more virtuous and industrious" black could allow them to flourish in their native environment and at the same time be a "civilizing" boon to Africa. There were hopes that free blacks in America could serve as missionaries in Africa.[14] Other proponents of colonization with less benign motives felt that as the number of free blacks increased, it would be difficult, if not impossible, to maintain complete discipline of black slaves.[15] Finley himself thought that slavery should be abolished because of its injurious effect on the country and that laws should be passed that made manumission of slaves easier. However, Finley, greatly concerned about racial "intermixture," felt that colonization was the best solution for all concerned.[16]

Finley garnered support from influential white citizens, including American statesman Henry Clay. Those in favor of colonization were a heterogeneous group with conflicting motivations. While some members of the ACS may have been motivated by humanitarian concerns, the majority were motivated by the conviction that free blacks must be separated from whites. After ten years the ACS began to decline and eventually disintegrated in the decade before the Civil War.[17] As problematic as the mixed motives of the group was, its failure can largely be attributed to the response of blacks opposed to the scheme.[18]

Initially, some blacks, such as Paul Cuffe of New England, viewed colonization with some interest. However, very soon blacks began to perceive the idea of colonization as a scheme to deport free blacks in order to ensure the existence of slavery. There was also the fear among blacks, despite assurances to the contrary, that colonization would be involuntary. Within ten years black opposition to colonization rose to a feverish pitch, although there were some blacks who, over time, again began to consider emigration when they became discouraged about the possibility of success in the black struggle for justice.[19] Nevertheless, for the most part, black abolitionist Martin R. Delaney's hostile characterization of colonization probably epitomizes the sentiments of most blacks of the time. He described the ACS as "anti-Christian in its character and misanthropic in its pretended sympathies." Delaney denounced the leaders of the colonization movement as "arrant hypocrites" and described the ACS itself as "one of the Negro's worst enemies."[20]

THE MILITANT PERIOD (1830–1840)

This period is marked by several events and developments within the antislavery movement. As many historians have noted, the character of the abolitionist movement became more confrontational with regard to slavery after 1830.[21] In 1829 David Walker's *Appeal* was published, and as a result, antislavery societies virtually disappeared in the South. After the insurrection of Nat Turner in Virginia in 1831 whatever antislavery sentiment there had been in the South became nonexistent. Another significant antislavery development was the formation of the American Anti-Slavery Society (AAS) in December 1833 in Philadelphia. Three blacks took part in the initial proceedings, and blacks participated in the organization of affiliates.[22] Such affiliates included women's auxiliaries and juvenile societies, which allowed women and children to participate in the black antislavery movement. Despite these developments, disputes emerged over the issue of immediate emancipation. Some within the wider movement grew impatient with the slow pace of progress. Others objected to the inclusion of women as leaders within the movement. Still others found it difficult to offer a strong critique of the church for not taking an unequivocal stand against slavery. Infighting among the leadership in the American Anti-Slavery Society would take its toll.

THE EARLY POLITICAL PERIOD (1840–1850)

The early political period saw the split of the AAS, the rise and fall of the Liberty Party, and an opportunity for black abolitionists to make fuller use of the resources from within their own community to battle the injustice of slavery. Out of the AAS, the American and Foreign Anti-Slavery Society emerged, with a program more narrowly limited to the abolition of slavery and without the leadership of William Lloyd Garrison, who remained with the AAS. An outgrowth of the new American and Foreign Anti-Slavery Society was the birth of the Liberty Party. John Hope Franklin characterizes the Liberty Party as the "nucleus" of the newly formed American and Foreign Anti-Slavery Society. This new political party, born out of frustration with the failure of either the Democratic or Whig party to take up the abolitionist cause, sought to combine its moral campaign for abolition with political influence through a new, uncorrupted political party. Unfortunately, the Liberty Party did not receive significant political support in the presidential campaigns of 1844 and 1848, despite the fact that millions of people were opposed to slavery by this point.

THE LATE POLITICAL PERIOD (1850–1860)

This period saw a number of significant political developments that would continue to stimulate antislavery activity in the face of growing opposition from Southern politicians supporting the slavocracy, culminating in the Civil War. The discovery of gold in California in 1848 and the rapid spread of populations in the Mexican cession led to inter-sectional strife over how the new territory should be divided into slave and free sections. Questions regarding the territories were debated by Congress in 1850. The ensuing conflict over the division of territory led to the Compromise of 1850. In its failure to settle the question of slavery once and for all, the Compromise left both the North and the South dissatisfied.

The passage of the Fugitive Slave Law, which was one of five measures known collectively as the Compromise of 1850,[23] provoked a fire storm of criticism. The Fugitive Slave Law[24] made the capture and return of escaped slaves a matter of federal law and rendered it virtually impossible for Northern states to evade their responsibilities under the Constitution.[25] The law denied an alleged fugitive the right to testify or a right to a trial by jury. The law also assumed that if a black person was labeled a fugitive, he or she was presumed guilty rather than innocent. Not only were real fugitives in jeopardy, but those blacks who either had been born free or who had been legally manumitted could and were "recaptured" and sent to the South without legal recourse. For understandable reasons, the passage of this new law not only created a "chorus of condemnation" from blacks, but it led to a black exodus from the United States to Canada that affected every Northern city with more than a few blacks.[26]

White abolitionists and those who heretofore had remained uninvolved in the issue of slavery viewed this law as a menacing encroachment of the Southern slavocracy that could have a detrimental effect upon the rights of *all* citizens because of the wide latitude given to law-enforcement officials for execution of the law. Prior to the passage of this law the rescue of fugitive slaves had been an activity conducted almost exclusively by blacks.[27] The Fugitive Slave Law of 1850 brought an influx of "new blood" into this work.[28] The zeal of slave holders to uphold fugitive slave laws led to greater defiance on the part of militant abolitionists, who were determined to assist runaway slaves.

The publication of Harriet Beecher Stowe's *Uncle Tom's Cabin* in 1852 demonstrated the power of literature to affect social change. Stowe was a participant in the antislavery movement of the 1850s.[29] Her novel sold more than 300,000 copies in its first year of publication.[30] With its story of extreme cruelty on the part of masters and overseers and its description of the suffering and privation of black slaves, it won thousands over to abolitionism and placed an even greater strain on inter-sectional relations.[31]

Another significant event in this phase of abolitionism involved the highest judiciary of the land. The Dred Scott decision of the U.S. Supreme Court (1857) created a new wave of militancy among black abolitionists. The reaction from the black community was sure and swift, condemning the decision as one that added insult to injury to the plight of blacks. The decision, which denied the citizenship of blacks, proclaimed that at the time the United States was founded blacks had no rights that the white man was bound to respect. At the annual meeting of the American Anti-Slavery Society in New York, Frederick Douglass characterized the decision as a "judicial incarnation of wolfishness" and the product of the "the Slaveholding wing of the Supreme Court."[32]

The final significant event in this period was the raid led by radical abolitionist John Brown at Harper's Ferry, Virginia (now West Virginia) in the fall of 1859. The raid of the government arsenal was intended to be a prelude to establishing a stronghold in the mountains in order to liberate the slaves.[33] Brown's unwavering principles of egalitarianism between the races and his unrelenting hatred of slavery earned him the kind of respect from blacks that few other reformers could claim.[34] Between the time that the raid was suppressed and surviving participants were captured and imprisoned pending a trial and subsequent execution, Brown received the sympathy and esteem of an overwhelming majority of black Americans, including noted black abolitionist James W. C. Pennington. Pennington published an editorial in a black newspaper in which he called for prayer in behalf of the hapless abolitionist.[35]

THE CIVIL WAR PERIOD (1860–1865)

This period marks the culmination of inter-sectional conflict over the issue of slavery and its impact upon the balance of power between the North and the South. The martyrdom of John Brown in late 1859 left the South terrified as it contemplated his violent attempt to liberate the slaves. The North was galvanized by Brown's deed, influencing many to support the Republican presidential ticket in 1860, which led to the election of Abraham Lincoln. Lincoln, though opposed to slavery, was not an ardent abolitionist. His election raised the issue of Southern secession to a higher level, but it was not seen as a major cause for celebration among abolitionists in the North, who were uncertain about his commitment to emancipation.

By mid-April 1861, weeks after Lincoln's first inauguration, Confederate forces fired on Fort Sumter; South Carolina seceded from the Union, thereby initiating the Civil War.[36] During the first two years of the war Lincoln sought to combine reluctant steps toward emancipation with a realizable plan of colonization. Lincoln, like many whites in the North, was convinced that whites and free blacks could not live together on an equal footing because of the widespread antipathy toward blacks. Consequently, the best solution for the "Negro problem" was believed to be a program of emancipation that included either the colonization or the emigration of blacks from the United States.

Abolitionists brought about some notable legislation and constitutional changes in regard to racial discrimination during the war and the Reconstruction period, though these changes were rarely enforced at the time.[37] Many abolitionists had been opposed to armed conflict as a means of securing abolition. However, once the war started, they maintained the conviction that it would bring about an end to slavery.[38] In the meantime, Lincoln and other Republicans sought to follow a prudent course between the demands of abolitionists and Northern racism.[39] The influence of abolitionists actively engaged in petition and speaking tours and educating the Northern public on emancipation placed pressure upon Lincoln to act decisively to free the slaves.[40] In September 1862 Lincoln issued a preliminary proclamation that declared that all slaves in areas still in rebellion on January 1, 1863, were "then, thenceforward, and forever free." Abolitionists' initial jubilation dissipated once they realized that the proclamation did not apply to those slaves in states that had *not* seceded from the Union and that once the war ended the proclamation could be challenged.[41] Consequently, abolitionists sought an abolition amendment. The Thirteenth Amendment was passed and ratified in 1865.

Abolitionists viewed the end of the war as a victory, for it was through their relentless pressure that public opinion had been swayed toward the ending of the institution of slavery. However, emancipation did not bring forth the thoroughgoing transformation of racial attitudes that would guarantee full equality for blacks, as black abolitionists had dearly hoped. White abolitionists, including William Lloyd Garrison, thought that the abolitionist struggle was over with the ratification of the Thirteenth Amendment in 1865, although they were aware that further work was needed in terms of the education, uplift, and securing of equal rights for freed blacks.[42] The abolitionist movement after 1865 lacked the necessary economic and political weapons needed to supplement the work of moral suasion and charitable relief that characterized early post–Civil War efforts in behalf of blacks by Northerners who had worked for abolition.[43]

The post–Civil War period launched Reconstruction, which was then followed by the withdrawal of federal troops from the South in 1877, the abandonment of blacks as wards of the nation, and the surrender of attempts to guarantee that freed blacks receive civil and political equality.[44] In the wake of Reconstruction, whites in the South resumed their position of domination over blacks. This led to another system of dehumanization that culminated in another major movement for full equality for blacks in the 1950s and 1960s. The central issue, which had not been adequately addressed by the emancipation of the nineteenth century, was the black quest for human dignity and justice. The modern civil rights movement underscored the conviction that the quest of the previous century had gone unfulfilled, despite the legal emancipation of black slaves.

Chapter 3

Abolitionism in Black and White

Abolitionists in Context

Gerald Sorin maintains that abolitionists tried to secure racial justice, to eliminate a deeply entrenched racism, and to lay the foundation for a society based on human relationships that transcended the "cash nexus"—a society structured to allow its members to fulfill their spiritual and moral potentialities.[1] This characterization of the movement's intent suggests a somewhat unified goal among abolitionists in general, though the means by which they attempted to achieve that goal could vary. Working from this assumption, some authors have attempted to classify the abolitionists by the means they used. Others have noted the difficulty of such an undertaking. Some have characterized certain white abolitionists as more concerned about their own civil liberties than those of free blacks. Others have contended that some black abolitionists were more concerned about immediate emancipation than the theological significance of slavery as a sin.

Herman E. Thomas, a scholar of African American religious history, argues that none of those interpretations adequately captures the nuances of perspectives within the movement. To avoid these oversimplifications, he proposes the use of a classification system for abolitionists developed by historian Aileen S. Kraditor, which identifies four categories of abolitionism designed to delineate some of the distinctions between white and black abolitionists.[2] However, before we look at those categories, it is helpful to examine briefly Kraditor's definition of an abolitionist.

KRADITOR'S CLASSIFICATION OF ABOLITIONISTS

Kraditor defines an abolitionist as "any man or woman who belonged to an antislavery society [between 1834 and 1850] . . . and who believed that slavery was a sin, that slaves should be freed immediately, and unconditionally, and without expatriation or compensation to the owners, and who subscribed at least in theory to the doctrine of race equality."[3] While this definition provides a starting point for defining an abolitionist, at various points it seems unnecessarily limiting. First, the period that she cites for abolitionism, 1834–1850, does not fully encompass the duration of the movement. It rules out any abolitionist activity in the latter part of the eighteenth century, thus excluding the work of Quakers and blacks who were engaged in abolitionist work prior to 1834. Additionally, by marking the close of abolition at 1850, she excludes the activity of abolitionists, both black and white, during the critical political years leading up to the Civil War.

A second limitation is her insistence upon formal membership in an antislavery society. It excludes the activity of those who acted to circumvent slavery through participation in the Underground Railroad, providing assistance to fugitive slaves, or taking part in informal activity in church groups not officially part of the recognized antislavery societies.

A third limitation is the requirement to support immediate, unconditional emancipation. Although the concept that an abolitionist believed that slaves should be freed unconditionally and immediately is useful, it becomes problematical in terms of how to characterize the Quakers, who, as early abolitionists, tended to be gradualists and sought an approach that would foster brotherhood between former masters and slaves rather than a purely adversarial relationship. Although there certainly were limits to the effectiveness of their approach, politically, the activity of the Quakers offered aid and succor to fugitives from the system.

A final limitation is Kraditor's requirement that abolitionists subscribe to racial equality ("at least in theory"). This requirement in her definition is problematical because a doctrine of racial equality should have been a nonnegotiable element in abolitionism, if one were to be understood as an abolitionist in a humanitarian sense. However, that said, if such a standard had been applied strictly, it would have eliminated a good number of white abolitionists as something other than "true" abolitionists, because they could not meet that standard.

Although Herman Thomas is aware of a number of these concerns with Kraditor's definition of an abolitionist, he finds her schema useful, nevertheless, and explains how certain well-known figures are categorized. There is value in identifying how Kraditor classifies these figures, because it does help to illumine some of the subtleties, shades of nuance, and overlap among them in a way that paints a fuller picture of the complexity of the movement—at least during a sixteen-year period in the early to mid-nineteenth century.

William Lloyd Garrison, a widely known white radical abolitionist and controversial figure in antislavery circles, is used as the standard for measuring abolitionist activity in Kraditor's schema. Her categories are determined by proximity or lack thereof to Garrison's approach to abolitionism. Kraditor devises four categories, noting distinctive aspects of an approach to abolitionism. Category one is identified as *Garrisonian*. A person classified as a Garrisonian supported Garrison's belief that an antislavery society should be broad, in the sense that it should include members with a variety of religious, social, and political views. The only element uniting abolitionists in this category is their devotion to abolitionist principles (as encompassed in Kraditor's definition of an abolitionist).

In contrast to the Garrisonians are the *anti-Garrisonians*. A person in this category narrowed the scope of antislavery activity to avoid alienating the general Northern public. Also, the anti-Garrisonians believed that "the [antislavery] societies should officially endorse political action." This position on politics generally occurred after 1839.

The third category is the *conservatives*. Those in this category took a sanguine view of Northern society in general, seeing it as essentially good, and maintained that the elimination of slavery was a move that would "preserve [society's] basically moral arrangements." "Kraditor's conservatives also believed that slavery was an evil that ought to be abolished, preferably by moral persuasion."[4]

The fourth category includes the *radicals*. Kraditor views a radical abolitionist as one who, like Garrison, "believed that American society, North as well as South, was fundamentally immoral, with slavery only the worst of its many sins, and who looked forward to a thorough-going change in its institutional structure and ideology."[5] Interestingly, William Lloyd Garrison himself would be classified not as a Garrisonian but as a radical.[6]

Thomas notes that Kraditor initially identified these four categories of abolitionism but later speaks more readily of two factions: the reformist and the radical. Thomas cautions that one must avoid conceiving these two groups as merely representing differences in degree, with both fundamentally heading in the same direction. Although on some issues this is true, the distinction between the reformist and the radical is starker on a fundamental point: the reformist sought to preserve and strengthen the American social order, while the radical was inclined to subvert that order and replace it with a new one.[7]

WHITE ABOLITIONISTS IN KRADITOR'S SYSTEM

Finding Kraditor's classifications useful, Herman Thomas applies them to James W. C. Pennington and Henry Highland Garnet, as well as using them to characterize the antislavery stance of several other abolitionists, white and black. Like Kraditor, Thomas uses William Lloyd Garrison as the standard, and abolitionists are categorized in terms of their proximity to Garrison. Garrison was motivated by a basic belief that slavery was wrong and a sin.[8] His goal was a perfect society, and he believed that the federal government was an immoral, imperfect institution that condoned and supported slavery. Accordingly, from his perspective abolitionists should not participate in the political process of the nation.

Thomas indicates that this "no government" stance was based upon Garrison's radical belief in a form of religious perfectionism, whereby a people wholly redeemed from iniquity would have no need of police, a penal code, or a dungeon. If society were reformed with perfection as its goal, then evils such as slavery would be destroyed. For Garrison, nonviolence was the only legitimate method; moral suasion was its best mode of application.[9] On this basis, Wendell Phillips, a Boston lawyer and abolitionist, would be classified as a Garrisonian.

Phillips refused to give allegiance to the federal government because he believed that it was founded upon a proslavery compact, that is, the U.S. Constitution. After studying a number of compromises, including the Three-Fifths Compromise, which legally sanctioned slavery, Phillips proposed the dissolution of the Union in 1856. He believed that the abolition of slavery would lead to this dissolution.[10] However, even though Phillips was a Garrisonian, his view of the Constitution did not preclude political activity. Phillips viewed alliances that did not compromise the principle of disunion as acceptable; thus, he could see disunionists working with proslavery people. But disunionists always had to be prepared to resign their position rather than act contrary to their principle. Phillips himself could not subscribe to Garrisonian non-resistance, though he was an ardent supporter of non-resistants. (A *non-resistant* was an individual Christian who "renounced all manifestations of force, including human government." Non-resistants believed that the only true government was the "government of God," which they argued would be established with the return of Christ.[11])

Lewis and Arthur Tappan were anti-Garrisonians. They agreed with Garrison that nonviolent action should be used in the fight against slavery. But Garrison wanted an immediate conversion of the American conscience to the cause of freedom. In contrast, the Tappans sought a gradual transformation of national sentiment on the matter. Thus, they advocated the use of the political process as a means of effecting the freedom of slaves and the attainment of equality for free blacks.[12] The Tappans supported the American Anti-Slavery Society (AAS) until 1839, when it adopted Garrison's "no-government" stance. In 1840 the Tappans and others formed the American and Foreign Anti-Slavery Society. This newer society supported the use of the ballot and moral persuasion against slavery. Since the Tappans favored political action and did not endorse violence, their strategy supported moral arguments and nonviolent political tactics in order to prick the conscience of the American public about the need for Christian antislavery activity.[13]

William Jay, the son of John Jay (the first chief justice of the U.S. Supreme Court), has been classified as a conservative abolitionist. A lawyer and then a judge, he believed that slavery was morally wrong. He also believed that the AAS should stick to a single cause: the abolition of slavery. Thus, he opposed a resolution passed at an AAS meeting that required its members to abstain from the use of products of slave labor. He objected to coercing others to obey a practice not addressed in the AAS's constitution. Jay favored unity and believed that discussion of controversial issues could not sustain that.

Herman Thomas indicates that Jay was also conservative in his interpretation of the U.S. Constitution on the issue of slavery, at least until the debate arose concerning the annexation of Texas. Prior to 1854, before the annexation of Texas, he maintained that the Constitution's toleration of slavery did not warrant dissolution of the Union. He believed that slavery would die because it was confined to the South. However, with the annexation of Texas he believed that there was "clear evidence" that slavery was not only alive but expanding. Thus, he took the position that "dissolution must take place, and the sooner the better."[14] For Jay, dissolution meant a nonviolent separation of the North from the South.

BLACK ABOLITIONISM IN KRADITOR'S SYSTEM

Thomas also finds Kraditor's categories useful as he examines the general black abolitionist position. Thomas has identified blacks in the ranks of Garrisonians, radicals, anti-Garrisonians, and conservatives. For example, Charles Lenox Remond, the first renowned African American abolitionist orator, was a Garrisonian. He advised blacks to disobey the laws of the land, or at least to ignore the Constitution. Remond took the position "no privileges, no pay"; he asserted that it was appropriate to withhold taxes from any institution that deprived him of its privileges and advantages, despite the cost of imprisonment or confiscation.[15] Remond not only encouraged acts of civil disobedience, but he also advocated the dissolution of the federal government, which he viewed as the primary perpetuator of slavery. He supported Garrison's motto: "No union with slave holders."[16] Like radicals and Garrisonians, Remond believed that the Union established by the Constitution was corrupt and should be dissolved. On that basis he opposed the Liberty Party, even though it was abolitionist in principle and worked to end slavery by political means. Remond maintained that all political parties were necessarily corrupt because their very existence was the result of compromise.[17]

On the other hand, James McCune Smith, a prominent black New York City physician, believed that political action was "absolutely essential for the abolition of slavery."[18] Smith is classified as an anti-Garrisonian because he favored political abolitionism.[19] According to Smith, "there is but one way to attack slavery through political action: it is to make it the sole idea of that political action. . . . Any other method would be as futile as the attempt to stop the slave trade and let slavery alone."[20] Smith maintained that since slavery had been established and legalized by the national government, it would have to be destroyed by the power that gave it legal status: the federal government.[21]

Thomas identifies William Whipper, a black lumberyard owner from Philadelphia, as a conservative abolitionist. Whipper believed that Northern society's moral arrangement was basically good and that the abolition of slavery would correct its deficiencies. Whipper, the son of a black servant and a white father, acknowledged that slavery was immoral but thought that it should be abolished by nonviolent action. He was an avid Quaker supporter of the American Peace Society. In 1837 he maintained that "abolitionists have been beaten and stoned, mobbed and persecuted from city to city, and never returned evil for evil."[22] Even though he insisted that slaves should not use violence to escape their enslavement, he did persuade the 1835 National Negro Convention to encourage blacks to disobey fugitive slave laws in a peaceful way.[23]

Whipper was also a popular Underground Railroad operator whose lumberyard was burned twice, probably because he had aided fugitives who were en route to Canada. Thomas indicates that Whipper leaned toward complete nonviolence and away from black-only organizations and political action because he believed that the existence of black churches and schools weakened the demand among whites for equality. Finally, Whipper believed that moral means was the best way to correct the sin of American society. He also felt that involvement with political parties, and federal, state and local agencies, constituted cooperation with evil.[24]

In his examination of Henry Highland Garnet, Thomas notes that Garnet supported violence, unlike the conservative Whipper. Garnet also believed that political action to abolish slavery and to achieve justice and equality was absolutely necessary.[25] Garnet was a radical who advocated the application of the Golden

Rule by slaves on an individual basis in order to obtain their freedom. Likening him to Garrison, Thomas maintains that Garnet believed that slavery was wrong and a sin. Garnet's goal was the liberation of slaves as a *precondition* for the establishment of equality in the human community.[26] Garnet appealed to slaves to rebel against their masters and "strike for their lives and liberties" with "resistance! resistance! RESISTANCE!" as their motto. Garnet was the first black man to join the Liberty Party. He also supported the Republican Party in 1856 as a way of seeking a political solution to slavery. However, he eventually became convinced that emigration was the best means of abolishing slavery in the United States.[27] In 1858 he was instrumental in organizing and bringing to public attention the African Civilization Society, which hoped to abolish slavery in the United States by bringing to Africa a new form of Christianity, science, and commerce. The hope was that those emigrants would bring progress to Africa through the use of free (black) labor.

Using Kraditor's schema, Thomas classifies James Pennington as an anti-Garrisonian, one of those who vehemently opposed slavery and caste, like Garrison, but who "saw themselves more as reformers within American religion and politics rather than as radicals who would subvert the social order and replace it with a new model."[28] Pennington is identified in particular with the "come-outers"—those who organized new churches and numerous institutions in religion, education, and politics based on "strict antislavery principles."[29] These Christian abolitionists were extremely critical of most religious organizations because they accommodated themselves to racism and slavery. They believed that evangelical Protestantism could be a source of *national* salvation. In his discussion Thomas extends the boundary of this category of abolitionism beyond 1850. He deals at length with Pennington's perspective on abolitionism and indicates that Pennington shared some tenets of each of Kraditor's categories. But Pennington basically endorsed political action and generally accepted Northern moral theory based primarily on scripture and natural reason. Consistent with the Garrisonians and the radicals, Pennington wanted to restructure society. However, unlike the Garrisonians and the radicals, Pennington accepted the theoretical principles of the Declaration of Independence and the Constitution.[30]

Thomas notes that, like some white abolitionists, black abolitionists agreed that slavery was morally wrong and should be abolished. Both races used a variety of tactics to achieve the goal of freedom for the slaves.[31] Black abolitionists could agree with the call for disunion from both the Garrisonians, like Wendell Phillips, and the conservatives, like John Jay, as long as subsequent action resulted in abolition of slavery. Thomas indicates that while Pennington endorsed the general goals of Garrison and the Tappans, he also pursued one of equal value: ending racial discrimination and caste. In addition to debating tactics among themselves and with whites, some black abolitionists had the added incentive of having been personal victims of slavery's many abuses.[32]

Aileen Kraditor's categorizations help flesh out some of the varying shades of abolitionism in general. However, in some ways they are less useful in relation to black abolitionists. One difficulty lies in setting up Garrison as the standard rather than using categories that address the completeness of goals. Perhaps a more helpful measure would distinguish between abolitionists who favored emancipation of slaves but could not embrace a doctrine of full equality and those who fought for both emancipation and equality. Another distinction is between those willing to endorse violence to achieve emancipation and those who insisted upon nonviolent means only. Yet another difference could be among abolitionists who endorsed *only* moral suasion as a means of abolition, those who sought political engagement *only*, and those who endorsed a combination of the two.

ELKINS'S CLASSIFICATION OF ABOLITIONISTS

Stanley M. Elkins offers yet another classification system for abolitionists based upon the adherents' antislavery sentiments as of 1835. The first category is *colonizationists*. Abolitionists identified as colonizationists supported the efforts of the American Colonization Society, which numbered among its prominent adherents James Madison, James Monroe, and Henry Clay. Society members proposed the deportation of free blacks to Liberia. As noted before, this plan was viewed favorably by Southerners who sought to safeguard slavery by ridding the country of free blacks who could influence slaves to protest their enslavement. The plan, promoted as an antislavery program, was viewed favorably by Northerners because it would make manumissions more feasible and more numerous.[33]

Elkins's second category is *philosophical abolitionism.* Philosophical abolitionists, including American religious leader William Ellery Channing, viewed slavery as an evil that should be abandoned, but they were not optimistic that it would happen immediately. Therefore, they gave attention to the improvement of the institution and of relations between master and slave.[34]

Elkins's third category is *gradual immediatism,* or "immediate emancipation gradually accomplished."[35] The nucleus of this category, which included the Tappan brothers, Theodore Weld, William Goodell, and James Birney, formed the AAS. Adherents to gradual immediatism believed that edicts of emancipation, promulgated immediately, might be followed by a series of gradual stages, such as peonage or apprenticeship, in hopes that slaves might ultimately be prepared for full civic status.[36]

Finally, Elkins's fourth category is *immediate and unqualified emancipation.* This doctrine was established in the early editions of William Lloyd Garrison's newspaper, *Liberator.* This position was upheld by Garrison and his followers.[37]

Elkins's more succinct classification of abolitionists has its benefits in terms of covering the range of positions with regard to abolitionism. However, his categorizations have the same problems associated with other forms of classification. The range of positions is more appropriate in terms of assessing the intellectual variations in the debates in white antislavery circles. A different classification system is needed to assess variations within black abolitionist circles. The debates governing white abolitionists were governed by beliefs about the propriety and the consequences of blacks and whites living within society on an equal footing. Their debates also centered on growing sectional conflicts between the North and South over economic and political power, and the effect slavery would have on the balance of power. The latter concern, if a concern at all for black abolitionists, was secondary or tertiary in relation to their concern about the welfare of free blacks and recently emancipated slaves.

DIFFICULTIES IN CLASSIFICATION

In reflecting upon the systems proposed by Kraditor and Elkins, we can say that each of these attempts at classification of abolitionists has some value. However, they fail to give consideration to the fact that oppressed and oppressor have different motives, approaches, and emphases, even when they attempt to work together toward a common goal. This is true because of the imbalance of power between them. Although members of the reforming society, who are also members of the oppressor class, may be seeking genuine reform, their economic, social, political, and psychological interests remain connected with the oppressor group to which they belong. Often religious and humanitarian impulses are not strong enough to override that connection.

This phenomenon was no different in the nineteenth-century abolitionist movement. As whites and blacks worked together, blacks found that they had different emphases than their white counterparts. Members belonging to the oppressor group will find the most expedient way of maintaining the balance of power and some measure of the status quo. They will quibble about, agonize over, and rationalize to find a path that does not precipitate more changes than they are willing to accept. Hence, the concern about maintaining unity; the worry about the impact of a large group of free blacks on their society; the desire to control emancipation in stages; and so on.

On the other hand, the oppressed are more impatient and unwilling to quibble over the means used to accomplish their goals. This impatience is due to their suffering. They already know what they need to relieve that suffering and what will make them whole. The oppressed want full measures, not half ones; understandably, they want change immediately. The oppressor and the oppressed, then, use distinct measures, and their approaches, and even their ultimate goals—their vision of the future society—may differ. Words such as *radical* or *conservative* in this context are used from the perspective of the group that wants to maintain its power, or at least wants to determine how far and how soon the sharing of power will take place. These differences in perspectives, motivations, and approaches make it difficult to devise a classification system that encompasses both groups in a way that allows for a fully comprehensive picture of the dynamics of a movement such as abolitionism.

In terms of an appropriate classification system to help us to understand the nature of black abolitionism and to encompass fully the styles of abolitionism among blacks engaged in the movement, a number of issues need to be considered apart from those raised in the classification systems just discussed. For example, what stance did various abolitionists take on whether they were viable in terms of promoting justice? That is, were they just in need of certain reforms or were American institutions so corrupted by racism that they were unreformable? Would nothing short of total restructuring of American institutions secure justice for blacks (a bit of the "non-Garrisonian vs. Garrisonian argument")?

Of course, there are additional matters to consider. Was emigration to Africa in the best interests of blacks, or was integration into American society as full citizens preferable? Was violence an acceptable tool for achieving emancipation or should the abolitionist insist on the adoption of an ethic of nonviolence? An issue that was debated well into the twentieth century, and which highlighted the difference in social philosophy between Booker T. Washington and Frederick Douglass, was whether emphasis should be placed on training blacks for trade and service jobs or whether classical education for free black youth and newly emancipated slaves was appropriate and more desirable. Another concern of black abolitionists in the late stages of abolitionism was whether abolitionists should concern themselves with blacks in North America only or whether blacks should pursue a trans-African approach to antislavery activities.

This critique of these classifications is not intended to dismiss their value in terms of helping us understand the nature of some of the distinctions and variations within abolitionism. However, in looking at black abolitionists different criteria might be applied. The criteria for assessing this form of abolitionism should arise out of the issues that the particular community feels are important to achieving its goals. Although black abolitionists shared a fair number of views that are relevant to Kraditor's or Elkins's classifications, certain key issues that were pertinent to black abolitionists are not addressed in those systems at all.

PART II

FREEDOM FIGHTERS AND THE QUEST

Chapter 4

David Walker

David Walker was born in Wilmington, North Carolina, in 1785. The son of a free woman and an enslaved father, he was considered free because of his mother's free status. (Black children born during slavery inherited the status of their mothers in North Carolina.) In this respect Walker's free-born status sets him apart from Pennington, Garnet, and Ward. Despite the fact that Walker was free, he was well-acquainted with the institution of slavery, for he traveled throughout the South and saw the brutality of the system firsthand. As a result of exposure to the institution as it affected blacks so negatively, he developed a bitter hatred for slavery.[1] Walker left North Carolina, spending some time in Philadelphia before he settled in Boston, where he established a small shop selling old and new clothes near the wharf. Self-taught and extensively read, he spent long hours studying and writing.[2]

His antislavery activities included his role as the Boston agent for *Freedom's Journal*, the weekly abolitionist newspaper published in New York by black journalists Samuel Cornish and John Russwurm. Later, Walker served as agent for Cornish's newspaper *Rights of All*. His other antislavery activities included attending local meetings and lecturing against slavery.[3] He also held membership in the Massachusetts General Colored Association, which had been founded in 1826 for the abolition of slavery and the racial improvement of blacks.[4]

The crown jewel of Walker's abolitionist activity is his self-published treatise *Appeal to the Coloured Citizens of the World*, better known simply as David Walker's *Appeal*. Among slave holders it was viewed as subversive and an incitement to revolution.[5] This characterization can certainly be debated, but the document itself is a work born of long reflection, based on Walker's observations of the conditions of Africans in American society and encounters with many of the leading freedom fighters, social thinkers, and abolitionists of his day.[6] Less than a year after the *Appeal's* initial publication in the fall of 1829, Walker was found dead in the doorway of his shop, under mysterious circumstances.[7] Although he did not live to see the waves of militant resistance that seized the abolitionist movement in later decades of the nineteenth century, the impact of the *Appeal* lived on.

A REBUKE OF HYPOCRISY

In the *Appeal* Walker highlights the irony that in a "Christian nation," black slaves were treated worse than any people ever enslaved by a "heathen" nation.[8] It was an insight that he sought to prove. This charge would be asserted time and again in the essay, as if to strengthen his indictment of slavery in America. It galled him that white Christians of America ("pretenders," he called them), "treat us more cruel and barbarous than any Heathen nation did any people whom it had subjected, or reduced to the same condition."[9]

He says his motive for speaking out is "to awake in the breasts of my afflicted, degraded and slumbering brethren, a spirit of inquiry and investigation respecting our miseries and wretchedness in this Republican Land of Liberty!!!!!"[10] The primary source for the miseries of blacks is "the inhuman system of slavery." He contends that slavery is motivated by "avaricious usurpers," thereby ascribing economic motives to the system. Avarice[11] and the pursuit of gain are behind this system of injustice.[12] Slavery is a system of greed because blacks are uncompensated for their labors.

This system of avarice was defended by leading American statesmen. In his treatise Walker spends considerable time attacking Thomas Jefferson, whom he assessed as an intelligent, gifted man, but one who erred greatly in his questioning of the full humanity of blacks.[13] The fact that a man of Jefferson's stature could lend credibility to the notion of black inferiority troubled Walker because Jefferson, as principal drafter of the Declaration of Independence and a former president of the Republic, had much influence on the thinking of white Americans.

In addition to criticizing statesmen who embody the political hypocrisy of slavery in a land that worships freedom, Walker offers strong criticism of blacks who submit willingly to tyrants, who help support the slave system, or who commit "treacherous" acts against their own by betraying blacks who seek to escape the system. To submit to tyrants is to resist God.[14] Walker does not subscribe to an ethic of nonviolence, arguing that it is morally appropriate to "deliver blows" in self-defense.[15] For him, self-defense is the will of God to work for the salvation of the "entire being" of blacks.

As much as Walker condemns blacks who impede the struggle for freedom, he reserves his harshest criticism for Christian preachers.[16] He notes that it was a preacher, the Catholic priest Bartolomé de Las Casas, who traveled with Christopher Columbus and proposed to Spaniards that they import Africans as slaves to the Americas in the sixteenth century.[17] Christian preachers have done what they could to hinder the evangelization of black slaves[18] and to thwart the efforts of blacks to pray and worship God. Christian preachers have also been derelict in their duty as prophetic witnesses by failing to preach against slavery and oppression.

Even schemes that involved the exportation of free slaves draw Walker's ire. Although he acknowledges that some lent support to the colonization plan with good intentions, Walker condemns the plan as "a diabolical scheme." Walker believes, as did many black abolitionists, that the ultimate goal of colonization is to preserve the institution of slavery in the United States. It is seen as an effort to separate free blacks from slaves in order that those who remained enslaved will be content with the institution and satisfied to remain in "ignorance and wretchedness" while they serve the slave holders and the children of slave holders. Walker contends that part of the wretchedness of the condition of blacks can be traced to the colonization movement.

Walker identifies the twofold nature of hypocrisy that allows white America to uphold the institution of slavery upon its shores. The first aspect of hypocrisy lies within the political realm. Insofar as this nation was established on the principles of liberty and justice for all, slavery is a peculiar institution that contradicts the ideal of freedom espoused by its citizens. Walker reminds Americans of the ideals found in the Declaration of Independence, using the language of the Declaration itself: "We hold these truths to be self-evident–that ALL men are created EQUAL! That *they are endowed by their creator with certain unalienable rights*, that among these are life, *liberty*, and the pursuit of happiness!!"[19]

He challenges white Americans to compare the language of the Declaration with the "cruelties and murders" inflicted by their ancestors and themselves. He challenges white Americans to consider how their own suffering under colonization under Great Britain could have been only "one hundredth part" as cruel and tyrannical as the sufferings of blacks under slavery. There is the sense that Walker is somewhat exasperated by the seeming inability of white Americans to recognize (and feel utter embarrassment by) the staggering contradiction between the ideals of Americans and their practice in relation to a segment of the human population.

The second aspect of hypocrisy that Walker criticizes is the religious realm of American society. Insofar as this nation has invoked Christian principles as a second foundation for the American way of life, slavery is a gross violation of Christ's "double commandment" to love God and neighbor (Mt 22:37–40; Mk 12:29–31; Lk 10:27). The nature of this aspect of Walker's critique of slavery is reinforced by his own Christian faith, which provides a theological foundation for his opposition to slavery. He affirms that the cries of the enslaved have been heard by the "God of justice" and that at some point in time blacks will be redeemed from their condition. Anticipating by more than one hundred years basic tenets of black theology, Walker affirms that the God of the oppressed is a God of justice. Walker denies vehemently the myth of the happy and contented slave. Theologically, slavery is problematic because it is a system in which human beings surrender themselves to human masters, when, in truth, God is our only master.

In contradistinction to the theological error of slavery on this point, Walker asserts a common humanity and explicitly affirms the full humanity of blacks.[20] He states, "If you will allow that we are men, who feel for each other, does not the blood of our fathers and of us their children cry aloud to the Lord of Sabaoth against you, for the cruelties and murders with which you have, and do continue to afflict us."[21] In a passionate, outraged cry,

Walker asks rhetorically, "Are we men!!–I ask you, O my brethren! Are we men? Did our Creator make us to be slaves to dust and ashes like ourselves?"[22] For Walker, to place blacks under involuntary subjugation is to deny their full humanity.[23]

If slavery represents a theological error, so does color prejudice. Walker asserts that those who harbor prejudice against blacks because of their skin color impugn the character of the God of justice and mercy. To attribute something wrong to dark pigmentation suggests that God has erred in the creation of black people. Walker dismisses those who hold such notion as "dreadfully deceived."[24]

THE SACREDNESS OF HUMANITY

Walker declares freedom as God-given and the fight for freedom a "heavenly cause" that should be defended. Although forced labor is bad enough, what makes slavery doubly egregious is the systematic denial of the full *personhood* of blacks, which adds to their misery and degradation.[25] Personally, Walker would prefer death to servile submission. Another theological reason Walker opposes slavery is that human beings belong to the Holy Spirit.[26] He thinks it unseemly that a vessel of the Spirit of God should be enslaved.

This sacredness of humanity is clearly denied by the institution of slavery, and that denial is manifest in the degradation of blacks under this oppressive system. Walker describes the full nature of the degradation blacks have experienced under slavery when he writes, with great passion:

Man, in all ages and all nations of the earth, is the same. Man is a peculiar creature–he is the image of his God, though he may be subjected to the most wretched condition upon earth, yet the spirit and feeling which constitute the creature, man, can never be entirely erased from his breast, because God who made him after his own image, planted it in his heart; he cannot get rid of it. The whites knowing this, they do not know what to do; they know that they have done us so much injury, they are afraid that we, being men, and not brutes, will retaliate. . . . They beat us inhumanely,

sometimes almost to death, for attempting to inform ourselves, by reading the Word of our Maker, and at the same
time tell us that we are beings void of intellect!!! . . . But
glory, honour and praise to Heaven's King that the sons
and daughters of Africa, will in spite of all the opposition of
their enemies, stand forth in all the dignity and glory that is
granted by the Lord to his creature man.[27]

Despite their dehumanizing mistreatment, Walker contends that
the essence of what makes one human, which is implanted by
God, stays intact. This explains the spirit of resistance that remains in the slave held in bondage. Bearing in mind the strength
of that spirit helps to sustain the slave.

Further, Walker insists that the situation of the slaves is not
hopeless, despite the bleakness of their condition:

They keep us miserable now, and call us their property, but
some of them will have enough of us by and by–their stom-
achs shall run over with us; they want us for their slaves,
and shall have us to their fill. We are all in the world together!!–I said above, because we cannot help ourselves,
(viz. we cannot help the whites murdering our mothers and
our wives) but this statement is incorrect–for we can help
ourselves; for, if we lay aside abject servility, and be determined to act like men, and not brutes–the murderers among
the whites would be afraid to show their cruel heads.[28]

Resistance is critical to put an end to the tyranny they face,
and Walker maintains that slaves have a responsibility as Christians to resist. He writes, "God will indeed, deliver you . . . from
your deplorable and wretched condition under the Christians of
America. I charge you this day before my God to lay no obstacle
in his way."[29] Elsewhere, he reiterates this idea:

For I believe that it is the will of the Lord that our greatest
happiness shall consist in working for the salvation of our
whole body. . . . I assure that God will accomplish it–if nothing else will answer, he will hurl tyrants and devils into *at-
oms* and make way for his people. But O my brethren! I say

unto you again, you must go to work and prepare the way of the Lord.[30]

Ultimately, Walker believes that it is up to blacks themselves to demonstrate and defend their full personhood.[31] He attacks the prejudice that fails to acknowledge their full humanity. He contends that in the enslavement of blacks, whites are guilty of nothing less than idolatry; that is, usurping the rightful place of God by their insistence upon exercising an illegitimate lordship over other human beings. To bolster his argument Walker appeals to morality as a standard by which one can judge inferiority and superiority and holds that by this standard, in terms of their treatment of blacks, whites have demonstrated *inferiority*, not superiority.[32] Walker views ignorance as a significant contribution to the state of the blacks of his day and argues that their wretchedness is not their "natural state." He rails against the practice of whites' denying blacks educational opportunities in both secular and religious matters.

SUMMARY OF WALKER'S CRITIQUE

In summary, Walker's convictions about the true nature of slavery are developed through his exposure to the institution as a youth, despite the fact that he himself held the status of free born. His encounter with slavery, as he saw the mistreatment of fellow blacks, fed a hatred toward it that fueled his passion to fight for the abolition of slavery. In the *Appeal*, the fruit of years of long study, reflection, and exposure to radical social thought, Walker offers a twofold indictment of America: the hypocrisy of its religious profession as Christian and its political ideals as a democratic republic that labels itself the land of liberty. This is a common refrain in abolitionists' (black and white) critique of American slavery. He emphasizes the degraded condition of slaves, rendered as beasts of burden, under an institution grounded in avarice. Walker highlights the theological error of slavery, condemning it as idolatrous, in conflict with the God of justice and a denial of the handiwork of the God who has implanted the divine image in all persons.

As problematic as the institution of slavery is as it works its way of death upon blacks, Walker does not view the situation with despair. He writes with great conviction that there *is* hope. The God of justice is on the side of the oppressed. Therefore, the Christian slave is *obligated* to resist and not to submit to the tyranny of a godless system. For Walker, the keys to restoration of the human dignity of blacks are religion (that is, the Christian faith) and education. Both faith and education are critical for succeeding in ending blacks' condition of degradation. For Walker, abolition of this horrendous system is clearly a question of the restoration of the human dignity of the black person.

Chapter 5

James W. C. Pennington

James Pembroke, who changed his name after his escape, was born a slave on the eastern shore of Maryland around the year 1807. His parents were owned by different masters. In his autobiographical slave narrative, he reveals that when he was four years old, he, his mother, and an older brother were sold to the son of his master, who moved to the western shore of Maryland.[1] Together with his mother and brother, he was separated from his father, and it is at this initial separation that he first became aware of the difficulties that slavery created for his family.

Although the family was subsequently reunited, Pembroke became increasingly aware of the dehumanizing character of the master-slave relationship. After overhearing his father being humiliated and savagely beaten by his master, he determined that he would not submit his "mind and spirit" to the servility demanded of slaves. This determination rendered Pembroke ripe for flight from his slave status. A short time after this incident involving his father, he made the decision to flee. The decision to do so caused him much anguish because he feared retribution against his family.

When Pembroke, now Pennington, eventually arrived in New York in the late 1820s, he was deeply perplexed by the condition of degraded slaves. This discomfort became more intense when he received religious instruction in the Christian faith. He experienced a period of acute spiritual conflict as he agonized over the suffering that slaves were forced to endure. He began to fast and pray on their behalf. Pennington perceived a critical link between personal salvation and emancipation. His conversion to Christianity led him to seek the help of God in behalf of the enslaved. Once his own salvation was assured, Pennington maintains, he began to turn his attention to addressing slavery as an expression of his newfound faith.[2] In his autobiographical narrative, he writes:

> [After conversion, slavery] seemed now . . . to be more hideous than ever. I saw it now as an evil under the moral government of God—as a sin not only against man, but also against God. The great and engrossing thought with me was, how shall I now employ my time and my talents so as to tell most effectually upon this system of wrong?[3]

Initially, Pennington considered attacking the institution of slavery "at the head," that is, by going to Africa where the slave trade began. However, as he found himself surrounded by recently freed slaves, following the abolition of slavery in New York in 1827, he came to believe that he could be of greater use in the abolitionist effort by assisting them. He became involved with the antislavery societies that were just being founded at that time.

Pennington penned his autobiography to "show God's handiwork with slaves" and to elicit support in behalf of fugitive slaves.[4] By telling his story, he sought to illustrate the difficulty that slaves encountered as they sought their liberty.[5] His critique of slavery was thoroughly grounded in his Christian faith, for he sought to educate Christians in general, and ministers in particular, to the sinful dimension of slavery. He explains: "The being of slavery, its soul and body, lives and moves in the chattel principle, the property principle, the bill of sale principle; the cart-whip, starvation, and nakedness, are its inevitable consequences to a greater or less extent, warring with the dispositions of men."[6]

This description of the institution was designed to rebuke those who spoke of slavery in terms of "kind masters," "Christians masters," "the mildest form of slavery," or "well-fed and clothed slaves," as though these descriptions mitigated the harmful impact of human bondage. Such minimization of slavery never ceased to outrage him. From his point of view the mildest form of slavery (if one could speak of such a thing) was comparatively the worst form because it rendered the slave "like a prisoner in chains awaiting his trial." Milder forms of the institution provided a false view of what slavery is "truly" like and failed to prepare the unsuspecting for circumstances in which a more malevolent master might be encountered in the future. Whether a slave had a kind or cruel master was a matter of irrelevance to Pennington.[7]

MORAL OBJECTIONS TO SLAVERY

Pennington has several moral objections to slavery. First, the nature of the system fosters immoral behavior. When he describes his own flight, he notes that in the course of seeking his freedom he was forced to lie and even to strike another human being in order to affect his escape. Resistance to the system forced him to commit acts that he would never have done otherwise, as a God-fearing man. He writes:

> The history of that day has never ceased to inspire me with a deeper hatred of slavery; I never recur to it but with the most intense horror at a system which can put a man not only in peril of liberty, limb, and life itself, but which may even send him in haste to the bar of God with a lie upon his lips. Whatever my readers may think, therefore, of the history of events of the day, do not admire in it the fabrications; but see in it the impediments that often fall into the pathway of the flying bondman. See how bloodhounds gratuitously chase, catch, and tempt him to shed blood and lie; how, when he would do good, evil is thrust upon him.[8]

A second objection to slavery lay in its destructiveness to black families. He asserts that one of the "chief annoyances" was that family members could be sold at any moment into more brutal circumstances arbitrarily and without warning. The anxiety surrounding such a change in one's living circumstances and the never-ending threat of separation from family members was a source of anguish for Pennington as he observed other blacks and as he recalled his own experience.

In addition to immorality and the destruction of familial ties, slavery promoted widespread ignorance in the slave population. Pennington viewed the impediments to education as tragic. In recalling receiving his first taste of education under the tutelage of Quakers, he engendered a great hatred of slavery because it stifled the ability of blacks to nurture and develop their capacity to learn. He writes rather poignantly: "I now began to see, for the first time, the extent of the mischief slavery had done to me. Twenty-one years of my life were gone, never again to return, and I was profoundly ignorant, comparatively, as a child five years old. This was painful, annoying, and humiliating in the extreme."[9]

The lost years under slavery haunted Pennington the rest of his life. He viewed that loss as the greatest robbery he suffered under the system. His discussion of that regret is worth noting in full:

> There is one sin that slavery committed against me, which I never can forgive. It robbed me of my education; the injury is irreparable; I feel the embarrassment more seriously now than I ever did before. It cost me two years' hard labour, after I fled, to unshackle my mind; it was three years before I had purged my language of slavery's idioms; it was four years before I had thrown off the crouching aspect of slavery; and now the evil that besets me is a great lack of general information, the foundation of which is most effectually laid in that part of life which I served as a slave. When I consider how much now, more than ever, depends upon sound and thorough education among coloured men, I am grievously overwhelmed with a sense of my deficiency, and more especially as I can never hope now to make it up.[10]

Pennington was shaken and appalled at his profound ignorance because of the condition of slavery under which he was born and reared. Apparently, the ignorance in which slaves were forced to exist contributed greatly to their degraded, dehumanized condition.

CONDEMNATION OF THE "CHATTEL PRINCIPLE"

As troublesome as these issues were for Pennington, the crucial aspect of slavery's moral offensiveness was what he calls the "chattel principle." Slavery transforms human beings into objects or expendable property. It denies the humanity of the slave. Pennington contends that the "chattel principle" is the crux of the slavery system; one cannot have slavery without it. In the end, both slave and master are degraded in the system. Because of this degradation one could not truthfully speak about "kind and Christian" masters. Ultimately, the slave system becomes the master of both.

The degradation of female slaves was of particular concern to Pennington. He notes the conditions under which female slaves served in some of the "milder" slave states, such as Maryland, Virginia, and Kentucky. He tell us that the females are "motherless, untrained in the natural graces, raised for the express purpose of supplying the market of a class of economical Louisian [sic] and Mississippi gentlemen, who do not wish to incur the expense of a legitimate family, and exposes the women to 'the most shameful degradation.'"[11]

Whether the slave was male or female, Pennington contends that the *chattel relation* robs the slave of his or her personhood, thereby, transferring self-ownership to another.[12] The chattel principle throws slaves' family history into "utter confusion" and leaves them without any record to which they may appeal in vindication of their character or honor. Instead of being able to chart a family tree, slaves find their names on a catalogue with the horses, cows, hogs, and dogs. The chattel principles robs slaves of their personhood *as a human being*. Pennington notes, "However humiliating and degrading it may be to his [a slave's] feelings to find his name written down among the beasts of the field, that is just the place, and the only place assigned to it by the chattel relation."[13]

Clearly, the nature of Pennington's critique of slavery rests with the inevitable dehumanizing dimension of the institution. He concludes his objection to slavery with a rhetorical plea: "I beg our Anglo-Saxon brethren to accustom themselves to think that we need something more than mere kindness. We ask for justice, truth, and honor as other men do."[14] This appeal identifies his remedy for the African American condition: not simply emancipation, but the kind of treatment rendered to other human beings. Perhaps as a defense against those who denied the sensitivity of blacks *as humans*, Pennington asserted that blacks were "widely awake" with regard to the degradation that they suffered "in having property vested in their persons," and that they were also conscious of the deep and corrupting disgrace of having their wives and children owned by other people.

SUMMARY OF PENNINGTON'S CRITIQUE

In summary, Pennington writes about the dehumanization of black life from the perspective of one who grew up as a slave but who managed to flee that kind of existence as a young man. The contrast between the life of a slave and the life of a (relatively) free man seemed so vast to him that he came to view eradicating the system of slavery and contributing to the elevation of black people as his personal vocation as a Christian. His slave narrative documents the degradation inherent in the institution of slavery, specifically citing the chattel principle as the essence of slavery. For Pennington, it was impossible to consider slavery in any other terms than as detrimental because systematic dehumanization of *both* the slave and the master was an inherent feature of the practice. A benevolent master did not make the system less malevolent, because ultimately the slave was transformed into and treated as property, a thing, denying his or her personhood. For Pennington, the best way to counteract the effects of this dehumanization of the slave was through conversion to the Christian faith and access to educational opportunities. Pennington makes an explicit connection between his own faith and the exercise of Christian discipleship through his antislavery activities. Although he emphasizes the incompatibility of slavery with Christianity, he, like Walker, recognizes the political hypocrisy of human bondage in a nation that champions liberty.

Chapter 6

Henry Highland Garnet

Like James W. C. Pennington, Henry Highland Garnet was a fugitive slave. Born in New Market, Kent County, Maryland, he fled as a young boy of nine with his family in 1824. Also like Pennington, Garnet initially fled to Pennsylvania, the first state north of Maryland that did not hold slaves. With the help of Thomas Garret, head of Pennsylvania's Underground Railroad, the Garnet family continued north to New York City. Garnet attended a school founded by the New York Manumission Society and a high school sponsored by blacks and designed to provide black youths with instruction in classical studies.[1]

Garnet continued to benefit from antislavery society sponsorship. He received further education in Canaan, New Hampshire, where he was among the first to attend an academy sponsored by the town's local antislavery society. It was during his student days there that he delivered his first formal speech before an abolitionist assembly.[2] As a result of the abolitionist focus of this assembly, the townspeople decided to close the school; whites were no longer willing to tolerate education for blacks, given the "subversive" activity of some of the school's students.[3] Harassment of Garnet and other students followed the school's closing, and the entire incident had a profound effect upon him. From this experience he concluded that the roots of black oppression were deep within white American institutions; thus, appeals to ethics, morality, and truth alone were insufficient to bring about black liberation. As long as such appeals conflicted with deeply entrenched economic and political interests, they were rendered meaningless.[4] From

71

Garnet's perspective, the elimination of oppression in society required a variety of tactics, no matter how drastic. As a result of his experience in New Hampshire, Garnet vowed that he would never celebrate the Fourth of July so long as slavery existed in America.[5] He and several other students formed a small society and resolved that when they completed their education they would go South and foment slave rebellions.[6] In 1836 Garnet continued his education at Oneida Theological Institute, where, two years earlier, students had formed what was believed to be the first antislavery society in the state of New York.[7] Eventually Garnet was ordained as a Presbyterian minister and served as pastor of a church in Troy.

Garnet's vocation as a minister was connected with his commitment to the struggle for black rights. In addition to his activities revolving around the African missionary movement and his work as a publisher of a newspaper dedicated to the cause of black liberation, Garnet used his talents as a writer and public speaker in the service of established abolitionist societies. Although a pastor himself, Garnet delivered lectures and speeches that were highly critical of American churches for their inaction in behalf of oppressed blacks.[8] In 1840 he attended the founding convention of the American and Foreign Anti-Slavery Society, whose members were opposed to the moral suasion approach of followers of William Lloyd Garrison. This New York–based abolitionist society, which favored direct political action to fight slavery (an approach which Garrisonians eschewed), included such figures as Gerrit Smith, William Goodell, and Arthur and Lewis Tappan.[9]

Garnet himself affirmed the goals of the Liberty Party. In 1842 he delivered one of the principal addresses at the party's convention in New York. After the convention the party formally engaged him to lecture among blacks throughout New York on the party's aims and goals.[10] Among the persistent themes of Garnet's speeches in behalf of the abolitionist cause was the importance of human dignity for blacks in the struggle for justice in America. The following analysis of a speech he delivered in 1843 illustrates his treatment of the theme of human dignity in relation to black justice.

SOLIDARITY WITH THE OPPRESSED

Garnet, speaking in Buffalo, New York, specifically addresses American slaves. In the speech he notes that free blacks in the

North, East, and West had been meeting at national conventions in order to sympathize with the slaves, but these freemen had never sent a direct word to the slaves themselves. Garnet states that he identifies with slaves and their suffering and asserts that he is writing to show the freemen's solidarity with the slaves.[11] He observes that the freemen are bound to the slaves not only through their common humanity but also because many of the freemen have relatives who remain in bondage.

Garnet states that despite the connection free blacks have with the slaves, there is a deep chasm that separates the one from the other. Nevertheless, he perceives the proverbial light at the end of the tunnel, for people are becoming wiser, the slavocracy is fading, and the slaves are becoming better informed. He rehearses the history of blacks in America, noting that they were brought to America without their consent. Furthermore, their dealings have been with those who profess to be Christians and yet exhibit the worst of human nature, including cruelty, avarice, and lust. Black people have come to America, he states, "not on the wings of liberty," but with broken hearts, doomed to "unrequited toil and deep degradation." He notes that since the first black arrived in America, generations of blacks since have remained in slavery. Despite early promises of ending the system, the cries of the oppressed have gone unheard and slavery has become more powerful as the church has stood by idly.[12] Garnet continues his sharp criticism of the church, blaming the "priests of the church" for their false prophetic witness, which has resulted in the triumph of the slavocracy. Indicting the church for its role in what amounts to a national tragedy, Garnet notes that nearly three million blacks have been prohibited by law and public opinion from reading the Bible.

THE NATURE OF BLACK OPPRESSION

Garnet contends that oppressors have destroyed the intellect of black folks and have participated in their ruin.[13] Further, they have participated in their own ruin, becoming "weak, sensual, and rapacious." In attacking the oppressors of blacks, he addresses, like many other black abolitionists, the political hypocrisy of American slave holders. He charges that colonists have placed the blame for slavery on England because at one time the English, too, practiced slavery. The colonists simply "inherited" a system that they now find themselves unable to eliminate. Ironically, the colonies ended up declaring their independence with a "striking document" that granted them the power of self-government, yet they did not end slavery.

Garnet extols the virtues of liberty and notes that unless the image of God is obliterated from the soul, *all* people cherish liberty.[14] He views liberty as a constitutive feature of human nature and asserts that in every mind "the good seeds of liberty" are planted; those who reduce their fellow man or woman into slavery commit the "highest crime against God and man."[15] Addressing the dehumanizing aspects of life as a slave, Garnet contends that the oppressor intends to make the slave a brute. He sets up a theological claim for resistance to slavery when he warns the slave, "To such Degradation it is sinful in the Extreme for you to make voluntary Submission."[16] Garnet argues that because slavery dehumanizes the slave and prevents the slave from meeting a human's obligations to God, it is not only fair but *necessary* for a slave to resist bondage. This is particularly true theologically because the divine commandments require that human beings obey God's command to love God supremely, to love their neighbor, to keep the Sabbath as a holy day, to search the scriptures, to raise their children with respect for the laws of God, and to worship only one God. However, the American system of slavery prevents the slave from obeying these commands. Garnet argues that the sad condition that slaves find themselves in does *not* destroy their moral obligation to God.[17]

RESISTANCE DEFENDED

Like Walker, Garnet contends that those who submit voluntarily to slavery place themselves in a position of disobedience to God. Emphasizing the spiritual harm of acquiescence to slavery, Garnet says to the slaves, "The diabolical injustice by which your liberties are cloven down, neither God, nor angels, or just men, command you to suffer for a single moment. Therefore it is your solemn and imperative duty to use every means, both [*sic*] moral, intellectual, and physical, that promises success."[18]

The passionate tone of his speech to slaves escalates as Garnet asserts that God will sanction any effort slaves make to free themselves from this tyrannical system. Just as it was wrong for the slaves' ancestors to be "stolen" from Africa, it is also wrong for slave holders to keep blacks enslaved. Therefore, slaves should resist just as their ancestors should have resisted the "first remorseless soul-thief" who came upon African shores. Garnet asserts that "the humblest peasant is as free in the sight of God as the proudest monarch that ever swayed a scepter. Liberty is a spirit sent out from God, and like its great Author, is no respecter of persons."[19]

Urging immediate action, Garnet tells the slaves that the time has come for them to act for themselves. Quoting an old saying, he says, "If hereditary bondmen would be free, they must themselves strike the first blow."[20] Garnet maintains that the slaves can plead their own cause and do the work of emancipation better than anyone. He notes that in theory, at least, the North has done more than the South to help end slavery; the South pleads that it needs "a more effectual door to be thrown open" to end it. Garnet indicates that the slaves themselves are that door. He implores them to think of the particulars of what they and their children have suffered at the hands of this system and then to tell the oppressors directly that they are "determined to be free."

In directing the slaves to begin to act to secure their liberation, Garnet tells the slaves that they should appeal to the slave holders' sense of justice. The slaves should tell their oppressors that they have no more right to oppress them than the oppressed have a right to oppress their oppressors. He entreats the slaves to "remove the grievous burdens which have been imposed" on them and to promise the landowners that they (the slaves) will renew their diligence in cultivating the soil if they are compensated for their services. The slaves should use language that their oppressors cannot misunderstand: *religious* language. The slaves should tell them of "the exceeding sinfulness of slavery, and of the future judgment, and of the righteous retribution of an indignant God."[21] He encourages the slaves to inform their oppressors that they want freedom and that nothing else will suffice. He states, "Do this, and for ever after cease to toil for the heartless tyrants, who give you no other reward but stripes and abuse." He tells the slaves that if the oppressors continue with "the work of death," then the slave holders will have to answer for that.[22]

Garnet recognizes that open resistance will engender conflict, and that such conflict might well lead to violence. He asserts that it is better to die immediately than to live as slaves and bring slavery's wretchedness on their posterity. Although Garnet is a devout Christian, he does not eschew violence in the service of the liberation struggle. He states, "However much you and all of us may desire it, there is not much hope of redemption without the shedding of blood. If you must bleed, let it all come at once—rather die freemen, than live to be the slaves."[23]

Because of their struggle in a patently immoral system, Garnet notes, slaves have become accustomed to hardship. In a sense, slavery has prepared them for any emergency, even the threat of death. Thus Garnet exhorts them, "Fellow men! Patient sufferers! Behold your dearest rights crushed to the earth! See your sons murdered, and your wives, mothers and sisters doomed to prostitution. In the name of the merciful God, and by all that life is worth, let it no longer be a debatable question whether it is better to choose liberty or death."[24] Like other black abolitionists, including David Walker, Garnet does not hesitate to appropriate the ultimatum of Patrick Henry.[25]

Garnet closes his speech to the slaves by recalling notable resisters such as Denmark Vesey, Nat Turner, Joseph Cinque of the Armistad, Madison Washington from New Orleans, Toussaint L'Ouverture, Lafayette, and Washington, as models of resistance:

> Brethren, arise, arise! Strike for your lives and liberties. Now is the day and the hour. Let every slave throughout this land do this and the days of slavery are numbered. You cannot be more oppressed than you have been—you cannot suffer greater cruelties than you have already. Rather die freemen than live to be slaves. Remember that you are four millions [*sic*]![26]

SUMMARY OF GARNET'S CRITIQUE

Garnet fled enslavement as a young boy, but his experience of the system was something he never forgot. He also knew first-hand the dangers inherent in living as a fugitive from slavery. The immediacy of those fears and his bitter experiences of discrimination gave him the courage to fight against those who upheld slavery in a "Christian" nation that boasted of itself as the "land of liberty." Garnet makes a strong connection between his ministry for the church and his antislavery activity in behalf of the black community. The theological harm of slavery–the denial of the dignity and worth of black people–is an important aspect of his critique of the institution. In slavery, the humanity of the enslaved is denied. The slave is treated as a brute devoid of human qualities. The remedy that could restore the dignity of blacks is religious and secular education. In terms of the battle for social justice, Garnet also insists upon the importance of political power as a necessary aid in the cause of abolition because the intransigence of white racism renders moral suasion less than effective.

Chapter 7

Samuel Ringgold Ward

Like Henry Highland Garnet, Samuel Ringgold Ward also escaped from slavery in Maryland with his parents. When the Wards fled to New York in 1826, they first lived with Garnet's parents.[1] Although his family was poor, Ward received an education and succeeded James W. C. Pennington as a teacher in a school for black children in New York. Ward also studied law, but he turned to the ministry after his conversion to Christianity in 1833. He was ordained and installed as pastor of an all-white congregation in a Congregational church in upstate New York in 1841. He viewed his two and a half-year tenure there as a good one, and he reluctantly surrendered his charge there when he became ill and could no longer preach.

Ward carried out his pastoral responsibilities concurrently with his antislavery activity. On the Fourth of July in 1834 an incident occurred that led him to commit himself to the antislavery cause. David Paul Brown was slated to deliver an antislavery speech at Chatham Chapel, but his efforts were thwarted by a mob instigated by city officials. Three days later blacks attempted to hold another meeting at Chatham Chapel, but it too met with harassment from a mob. Ward and several other blacks remained behind after the crowd was dispersed, and a group of whites returned and attacked them. Police arrested the blacks, including Ward, while their white attackers went free. Ward asserts that his own "oath of allegiance to the antislavery cause was taken in that [jail] cell on the 7th of July 1834."[2]

He became a traveling agent of the American Anti-Slavery Society, as well as the New York Anti-Slavery Society. He believed that antislavery work was his "life vocation," regardless of the occupations he held. Antislavery activity was a salient feature of his Christian praxis. In his autobiography he writes, "I regard all the upright demeanour, gentlemanly bearing, Christian character, social progress, and material prosperity, of every coloured man, especially if he be a native of the United States, as, in its kind, anti-slavery labour."[3]

His antislavery activity included speaking engagements in the United States and abroad; membership in the Liberty Party; the editing and proprietorship of two newspapers (which folded); and involvement in a notorious Fugitive Slave Law case in Syracuse in late 1851. Because of his involvement in the "Jerry rescue case," Ward was forced to move to Canada to escape prosecution.

THE SPECTER OF "NEGRO-HATE"

Ward's autobiography chronicles his antislavery experiences in the United States, Canada, and abroad and provides the context for his views about slavery and racism in America. His life-long concern about racism and its impact on African Americans is clearly evident in this text. His hatred of slavery lies principally with its dehumanization of the slave. Of racism's impact on black youth in New York, which he calls "Negro hate," he writes, "Added to poverty . . . in the case of a black lad in that city . . . is the ever-present, ever-crushing Negro-hate, which hedges up his path, discourages his efforts, damps his ardour, blasts his hopes, and embitters his spirits [*sic*]."[4]

He muses that the damage to the psyche from racism was such that it was a wonder that "the mass of us are not either depressed into idiocy or excited into demons."[5] Yet, he maintains, given the suffering they have had to endure under the system of slavery, blacks "spoke mildly" of their oppressors, as a general rule. Despite being excluded from fellowship with whites and being constantly disparaged because of prejudice, most blacks were not rendered hateful by the experience. Ward concedes that he as well as other blacks had been "stifled" in their effort to improve themselves and fulfill their potential. He notes the irony of encountering ostracism and flagrant racism even in the church, where the same degradation was played out in "the Negro pew."[6]

Ward's audience for his autobiographical account includes overseas readers and so he is quite detailed and expansive in his description of slavery in the United States. He wants to thoroughly acquaint his readers with the real nature of his opposition to the institution of slavery. He addresses racism at length because of its deleterious effect upon the *personhood* of the slave:

> The enemies of the Negro deny his capacity for improvement or progress; they say he is deficient in morals, manners, intellect, and character. Upon that assertion they base the American doctrine, proclaimed with all effrontery, that the Negro is neither fit for nor entitled to the rights, immunities and privileges, which the same parties say belong naturally to *all men*; indeed, some of them go so far as to deny that the Negro belongs to the human family.[7]

The comprehensive denigration of the capacity of blacks to participate as human beings in American society is the crux of his dispute with racism and the American system of slavery. He also observes the political hypocrisy of white Americans, just as other black abolitionists have.

Ward makes known a couple of ironies about slavery in America, which he points out in his discussion of the black experience. First, the discrimination that he and other blacks have experienced has not been limited to slave holders, for the worst of these offenses has occurred in *non*-slave-holding states.[8] Second, there is a troubling perversity of the American slavery system on familial affairs, for American slave holders are the worst and cruelest to their own mulatto children and other slaves. As he reflects upon these ironies, he wrestles with the cause of racism:

> It is quite true, that nowhere in the world has the Negro so bitter, so relentless enemies, as are the Americans; but it is not because of the existence of slavery, nor of the evil character or the lack of capacity on the part of the Negro. But, whatever is or is not the cause of it, there stands the fact; and this feeling is so universal that one almost regards "American" and "Negro-hater" as synonymous terms.[9]

Ultimately, he concludes the cause is unknown; however, his indictment of racism in America is complete.

RACISM AND THE CHRISTIAN CHURCH

His indictment of the United States extends to the Christian church in America. He argues that one would expect Christianity gradually to undermine and overthrow customs and superstitions and prejudices that are unchristian in character. However, he contends, often the *clergy* are the champions of Negrophobia. As a pastor and preacher of the Christian gospel, the failure of Christians to live up to the injunction of Jesus Christ to love God and love neighbor as oneself is particularly troubling. Ward's way of making sense of this phenomenon is to distinguish between *religion* and *Christianity*. Religion, he argues, should be substituted for Christianity in the American context. Religion comes from humankind and, as such, it is capable of eliciting hatred from its adherents. However, Christianity cannot lead people to hatred; it is always from God, and like God, it is love.[10] From his own experience and deep conviction, he contends that the oppression and the maltreatment of blacks is not merely

> an ugly excrescence upon American *religion*—not a blot upon it, not even an anomaly, a contradiction, and an admitted imperfection, a deplored weakness—a lamented form of indwelling, an easily besetting, sin; no, it is a part and parcel of it, a cardinal principle, a *sine qua non*, a cherished defended keystone, a cornerstone, of American faith.[11]

Ward views racism against blacks as not only a matter of "faith" but a significant feature of practice as well—something in which "an overwhelming majority" of whites are engaged.[12] In light of the scope of the problem, antislavery labor is "manifestly the refutation of all this miserable nonsense and heresy—for [slavery] is both."[13] By positing racism as a faith, Ward offers a theological critique of white supremacy, and this buttresses his argument with regard to the failure of the Christian Church to address the problem of slavery.

He is disappointed with most Christian denominations, noting that one-sixth of all slave holders belong to the Methodist, Baptist, Episcopal, and Presbyterian denominations. In his criticism of several Christian denominations he does not spare his own—the Congregational churches. Congregationalists were spiritual descendants of the Puritans; Ward charges that the Puritans were "lacking" in terms of any commitment to abolitionism.[14] The only denominations that he recognizes as offering opposition to slavery are the Quakers and the Free-Will Baptists.

Ward's condemnation does not rest with the Christian church alone but extends to benevolent societies under Christian auspices. He contends that these organizations not only have failed to interfere with slavery but actually seemed to pander to it.[15] The American Bible Society, the American Sunday School Union, and the American Board of Commissioners for Foreign Missions are singled out for particular criticism. Ward appears puzzled that slave holders could be members and officers of the American Bible Society, when slavery "forbids the searching of the Scriptures, which Christ enjoins," while at the same time these same slave owners could pledge to give the scriptures to every family in the Union.[16]

Ward addresses the varied rationale slave holders used to defend slavery and notes with some disdain their argument that non-slave-holding Christians should not challenge their slave-holding brethren because the latter are "good Christians." Slave holders want to enslave without impunity, as long as they treat their slaves "well" and appear pious in terms of their church standing (that is, their conversation is acceptable, their doctrine sound, and they are "correct" in matters other than slavery). Ward dismisses such arguments within the Christian community as problematical. Whether some Christians denied the sinfulness of slavery or hid behind the faults of abolitionists or defended slave holding from the Bible or from a desire to maintain harmony at any cost, the moral degradation might be viewed as subtle but the effects were deleterious just the same. In a critical vein, he writes:

> Let it not be forgotten, however, that behind all this—and going very far, I think, to explain it—is the contempt they all alike maintain towards the Negro. Surely, if they believed him to be an *equal brother man*, such miserable pretexts for,

and defences of, the doing of the mightiest wrongs against him, would never for a moment be thought of.[17]

Thus, for Ward, the excuses given for failing to condemn slavery conceal a deep theological flaw. If the full humanity of blacks is recognized, the immorality of the excuses would be revealed for what they were.

Ward maintains that true abolitionists have come to identify the genuine intrinsic nature and character of slavery. He writes, "Not in the abstract, but in the concrete—not as one might imagine it to be, but as it *is*—not as it was (or was not) two thousand years ago, more or less, but as it is *to-day*—its brutalizing, chattelizing; buying, selling, the image of God and the members of Christ's body; its adultery, fornication, incest."[18]

The distinction between assessing the immorality of slavery in terms of the concrete, rather than the abstract, was an important one for Ward and for many other black abolitionists. Black abolitionists sometimes grew impatient with white abolitionists for a tendency to view slavery in the abstract, without thinking of its impact on flesh-and-blood human beings.

In noting the theological implications of slavery, Ward highlights the dehumanizing aspects of American slavery and also distinguishes it from milder forms that may have been practiced in earlier times or in other civilizations. He views American slavery as particularly egregious from a theological perspective. It violates the Ten Commandments and denies the biblical law of love (love of God and love of neighbor). That being the case, he is left to wonder why it is so difficult for opponents of abolition to recognize the *sinfulness* of slavery. He asserts that abolitionists have to contend with those who maintain that the issue of slavery is not part of the business of the church, that it is not the place of "benevolent handmaids" to speak against existing social and political evils. Yet, the problem *has* infected the church, so much so that the American church itself is a bulwark of slavery. Abolitionists, he argues, have to challenge proslavery folk who contend that there are sins that the church and the pulpit should not and need not rebuke. The task of the abolitionist is to respond that the true prophets of old spoke about sin "in season and out of season."[19] For Ward, this was the state of the debate between abolitionists and their opponents in 1839, and it is still true as of 1855 (the year his autobiography was first published).

Ward contends that the American proslavery church has a false Christ, one who would die for the human race yet authorize the exclusion of blacks from this common salvation.[20] He questions the character of a god who would give a moral code from Sinai and then authorize one-fourth of those upon whom he makes that law binding to violate and trample underfoot every precept and principle of that code, harming the other three-fourths of their fellow human beings.[21] He concludes with an attack upon the purity of the church that "smiles upon, fondles, caresses, protects, and rejoices to defend a system" that would leave 1.75 million women to the "unbridled lusts of the men who hold despotic power over them."[22] Such a false religion, he contends, is an abomination and cannot be viewed as Christian.

After outlining the corruption of the American church and its people of faith, he notes that some abolitionists question whether such a church can be reformed. Ward believes that it can be. He then defines the issue as he understands it:

> It is not whether some men have wisely or unwisely pleaded this cause, nor whether their measures were commendable or not; not merely, what shall be done with the Negro? It is, shall religion, pure and undefiled, prevail in the land; or shall a corrupt, spurious, human system, dishonouring to God and oppressive to man, have the prevalence?[23]

THE POLITICAL DIMENSION OF ABOLITIONISM

Not only does Ward offer a thorough religious critique of slavery, but he also addresses the political dimension and outlines how the abolitionists of his day began to determine the degree to which they could wield their political power over the question of slavery. The politically active abolitionists felt that the Democratic and Whig parties had departed from the maxims of democracy and republicanism, just as the churches had strayed from the gospel. These two political parties, which had two-thirds of the votes between them, were heavily controlled by their Southern members. The largest share of the entire suffrage was Southern.

Southerners had obtained the highest political offices and, Ward contends, were wielding undue, disproportionate power to secure the interests of slavery.[24] In this context, in order for Northerners to secure power, they had to be "free from the taint" of abolitionism.[25] Meanwhile, in Northern localities "the friends and members" of these parties sought to "cajole and seduce" abolitionists into voting with their party, claiming that to do so would be more favorable to the antislavery cause than to its opponent, "while manifestly *both* were the tools and the props of the slave powers."[26]

Ward argues that abolitionists must recognize what is going on and either refrain from voting altogether (a position of staunch Garrisonians) or form a political party on antislavery principles. There were abolitionists who opted for the latter. The Liberty Party was formed in August 1840 at Syracuse. It was at this time that Ward became a member of a political party for the first time and cast his first vote. He devoted his political activities to that party for eleven years, before his abrupt departure to Canada.

The abolitionists who became part of the Liberty Party saw the government and political parties as false to their own sworn principles of freedom and democracy, just as the churches had trampled under foot the fundamental principles of Christianity. The government and political parties departed from the U.S. Constitution, which Ward maintains was made "to secure the blessings of liberty," and which ordained that "no man shall be deprived of liberty without due process of law."[27] In support of this contention, Ward writes:

> The Whigs denied the faith of their revolutionary fathers, whose Whiggism was but another name for self-sacrificing love of liberty. The Democrats, claiming Jefferson as their father and boasting of his having written the Declaration of Independence, hated nothing so intensely as Jefferson's writings against slavery—and that very Declaration of Independence, when, among "ALL MEN" in it declared to be entitled by God to the *unalienable* right to liberty, Negroes were said to be included.[28]

He asserts that both parties professed to be admirers of the great Washington but neither of them coveted the opportunity of using political power against slavery, as he wished to do in his native State.[29]

Ward sets forth the aim of the politically active abolitionists. They want to ensure a simple application of the principles of the Declaration of Independence to blacks as well as whites, and they want to guarantee that the former should share the same benefits secured through the U.S. Constitution as the latter.[30] The political abolitionists take the position that the Declaration says that the right of man to liberty is *unalienable,* and that no enactments, constitutions—not even consent of man himself or any combination of men—can alienate that which is by God's fiat made *unalienable.* For them, the basic principle is the *unalienable* right of man "to life, liberty, and the pursuit of happiness." Ward believes that as an agent of the New York State Anti-Slavery Society, he has a duty to devote himself to those political and religious principles.

As an antislavery activist Ward encountered those who were as aware as he that slavery encroached upon the political rights of American citizenry. It encroached upon the right of petition, freedom of the press, freedom of speech; it included the whipping, tarring and feathering, and lynching of *white* abolitionists in the South. But again, what he found most troubling was the way in which slavery deformed the personhood of black slaves. Moreover, he argues, this deformation of personhood also extended to white slave holders. Slavery jeopardizes and destroys the liberties of anyone it can crush as it victim. Politically active abolitionists such as Ward viewed the real political issue not as whether the black man's slavery should be perpetuated but as whether the freedom of *any* American can be permanent if slavery is allowed to exist.[31] Ward and others understood that the impact of slavery was broad, affecting all classes, involving the fate of everyone, and that it had the potential to undermine the basis of the nation's best institutions, including the whole range of American rights and the root of all constitutional government.

In response to those Christians who did not agree with his abolitionist stance, he offered these criteria for judging his abolitionist principles: whether the abolitionist doctrines agreed with the Bible, whether they were consistent with the law of love; and (more to the point) whether they were "part and parcel of what Jesus taught." He begged others to employ the same criteria for judging his antislavery work.[32]

RACIAL UPLIFT

Ward contends that the cure of the problem of slavery involves not just lecturing, holding antislavery conventions, distributing antislavery tracts, maintaining antislavery societies, and editing antislavery journals. Ward acknowledges that these common abolitionist activities are "right and necessary in themselves" but that the cultivation of all the upward tendencies in black people are also important.[33] Expert black cordwainers, blacksmiths, mechanics, artisans, teachers, lawyers, doctors, farmers, and ministers are required to use their vocations to demonstrate that Negrophobia is based upon lies about the capabilities of African Americans. In fact, all black labor is antislavery labor, for as a man or woman, a Christian, and especially as an *African* American, one's life ought to be an antislavery life.[34]

Unlike Walker and Garnet, in his discussion of his abolitionist experiences in the United States Ward gives no indication that he would defend the use of force to achieve success in the struggle for black justice. As a pastor he seems to have a strong identification with Jesus, who preached against nonviolence in the Sermon on the Mount. Despite the provocation that slavery exacts upon blacks, Ward eschews the adoption of hatred in response to ill-treatment. He concedes, though, that there is a "constant" temptation for blacks to hate whites.[35] But he argues that, natural and understandable as that emotion might be, it is important to remind his fellow blacks of the manner in which Jesus Christ was treated by those for whom he died (including blacks). It is also necessary to draw their attention to the fact that "in the face of bad social customs, education, and religion, God had indeed enabled *some whites* to do and endure all things for our cause, in its connection with their own."[36] He urges blacks to forgive as Christ has forgiven, for the sake of their souls. To surrender to racial hatred in response to legitimate grievances is to endanger one's own spiritual condition. Thus, he states that he prays that his people will be saved from that hatred.

When Ward pleads before whites in his antislavery activities, he avoids ever asking for pity for blacks, even as he faithfully depicts their suffering under slavery and the injustice done to the "nominally free."[37] This is because Ward does not wish to foster a victim cult among black people, despite their legitimate, soul-burdening grievances. To seek pity is to compromise self-respect; it would degrade his people if he were to ask for pity from their oppressors. Ward is aware that some abolitionists have sought pity in behalf of the cause, and he has never censured them, though he has avoided resorting to those tactics himself.

Ward contends that in his antislavery activity he ultimately seeks "even-handed justice" for blacks and asserts that blacks claim nothing more than everyone's birthright *as a human being.* He explains:

> What the Negro needs is, what belongs to him—what has been ruthlessly torn from him—and what is, by consent of a despotic democracy and a Christless religion, withholden from him, guiltily, perseveringly. When he shall have that restored, he can acquire *pity* enough, and all the sympathy he needs, cheap wares as they are; but to ask for them instead of his rights was never my calling.[38]

Interestingly, Ward also maintains that he could also not degrade himself by arguing the *equality* of blacks with whites, for in his private opinion, to say that blacks are equal morally to whites is "to say but very little"[39]:

> The cool impudence, and dastardly cowardice, of denying a black a seat in most of their colleges and academies, and literary and scientific institutions, from one end of the republic to the other; and, in like manner, shutting him out of most of the honourable and lucrative trades and professions, dooming him to be a mere "hewer of wood and drawer of water"—discouraging every effort he makes to elevate himself—and then declaring the Negro to be naturally, morally, intellectually, or socially, inferior to the white—have neither parallel nor existence outside of that head-quarters of injustice to the Negro, the United States of America.[40]

Although in his autobiography Ward strongly condemns white racism, and is determined to speak a prophetic word against it and against the institution of slavery, he also delivers a word of responsibility to black people. He believes that they have an important role to play in combating the deleterious effects of the system. He states that their role is to

> do the thing you do in the best possible manner: if you shoe a horse, do it so that no white man can improve it; if you plough a furrow, let it be ploughed to perfection's point; if you make a shoe, make it to bespeak further patronage from the fortunate wearer of it; if you shave a man, impress him with the idea that *such* shaving is a rare luxury; if you do no more than black his boots, send him out of your boot-black shop looking towards his feet, divided in his admiration as between the blacking and the perfection of its application.[41]

Furthermore, he exhorts, were free blacks to "do no more than simply improve themselves, without exhibiting the lofty patriotism which now so nobly prompts them to efforts for self-elevation, their gradual improvement would draw toward them the gaze, perhaps the admiration, of all the Old World."[42]

A FUGITIVE TWICE OVER

Ward's antislavery activities forced him to leave the United States rather abruptly in 1851 in the wake of his involvement in the escape of a mulatto slave who had been recaptured under the provisions of the 1850 Fugitive Slave Law. Because of the possibility of capture without due process of law, the Fugitive Slave Law evoked fear not only in the hearts of fugitive slaves but also the hearts of free African Americans.[43] Ward met with "Jerry," the mulatto slave, while Jerry was jailed. He was profoundly affected by the sight of this man who was condemned for his love of liberty. Ward writes movingly that never before had the talk about liberty in America and the profession of Christian faith made him feel that these things were a "hollow mockery."[44] He maintains that for the first time he saw how deeply the country was gripped by the slave power. It was also the first time that he knew the depths of degradation present in a professed freeman of the Northern states.[45] Ward spoke on behalf of the fugitive slave, and a sympathetic mob secured Jerry's escape. Because his participation was noted in a newspaper account of the incident, Ward was subject to be tried for treason. He fled to Canada, and a month or two later his family followed him. Fortunately, his abrupt departure from the United States did not end his antislavery labors.

SUMMARY OF WARD'S CRITIQUE

Ward's personal testimony of life as a slave, a fugitive, and an antislavery activist mirrors the experiences of other black abolitionists. However, he is particularly evocative as he recounts the deep spiritual and emotional harm that recipients of "Negro-hatred" encountered in the North as well as the South. He also addresses at some length the difficult challenge of marshaling a Christian response to egregiously unchristian conduct. Ward's Christian faith serves as the foundation for his antislavery activity. His faith is also the resource that sustains him in the arduous and sometimes discouraging struggle for justice. It also provides him with a strong ethic that precludes retaliation or ill-will toward one's oppressor, no matter how "natural" that reaction to provocation. Education is an important tool for blacks as they recover from the degradation of slavery. We can also see from Ward's story several other important elements required to restore black dignity. One is the cultivation of useful skills to debunk the claims of racists that blacks are incapable of anything other than service to whites. Another tool for use in the struggle for justice is political participation.

As was often the case with other abolitionists, Ward notes the political hypocrisy in America, the "land of liberty," as well as the religious hypocrisy of a nation that professes to be Christian. Ward views slavery as a sin and denounces the American church for its idolatry, for it worships a false Christ. He is also critical of the church and benevolent societies because of their insistence on maintaining harmony at all costs, by avoiding the issue of slavery. Ward maintains that the crux of the failure of the church and benevolent societies to condemn slavery is racism, with its denial of the full humanity of blacks.

Chapter 8

Black Abolitionism as a Quest for Human Dignity

From an examination of the writings of each of the four freedom fighters, set within the context of their personal lives, we find common themes that help to frame a portrait of the black abolitionist during a critical period of the movement: recognition of the evil of slavery and a deep antipathy toward the system; emphasis on the importance of secular and religious education of blacks to mitigate the effects of slavery; the view that resistance to slavery was justified, with conviction that such resistance had divine sanction; exposure of the political and religious hypocrisy of America; and a clear vision that restoration of black dignity was part and parcel of emancipation.

THE EVIL OF SLAVERY

Walker, Pennington, Garnet, and Ward all bear witness to the evil of slavery. Their understanding of Christian faith helped to provide a theological framework for understanding slavery as sin. They affirmed that all human beings are created in the image of God, that Christ died for the sins of *all*, and that all persons are subject to the law of love, namely, the requirement to love one's neighbor as oneself. Because there is one human family, and blacks are full members of that family under God, the buying and selling of slaves, the mistreatment of them, and the denial of the full humanity of black people constituted a sin of which America needed to repent. Each of the four men expresses a deep antipathy toward the institution of slavery, challenging the delusional notion that blacks were *especially* suited to slavery and that they were "happy" under that system. The passion with which each of these authors speaks about his personal experience of slavery and/ or his observations of it in the course of his travels barely conceals a rage that threatens to smother the Christian charity each one wished to convey as he launched his prophetic denunciations of "Christian" America.

THE IMPORTANCE OF EDUCATION

Each of the four expended tremendous effort to educate himself as part of the process of reversing the effects of slavery. Walker was self-taught. However, Pennington, Garnet, and Ward were educated in schools once they made their way North. Pennington, so desirous of receiving advanced education, attended lectures *outside* the classroom at Yale Divinity School because racial prejudice precluded his being able to sit in the same classroom with white students. The lost years of his youth haunted Pennington; he viewed those years in which he had been denied an education as the worst effect of slavery. All four authors were convinced of the necessity of educating blacks. Both Pennington and Garnet taught in black schools. Pennington, Garnet, and Ward also felt called to the Christian ministry and undertook studies to prepare themselves to serve in congregations. However, each understood his ministerial vocation in broader terms than fulfilling a pastorate with a single congregation. All viewed their antislavery activities as an important dimension of their Christian ministry. They saw no distinction between their profession of Christian faith and their active engagement in abolitionist endeavors. In fact, all four understood their abolitionist activities as concrete expressions of Christian faith.

RESISTANCE TO SLAVERY JUSTIFIED

Walker, Pennington, Garnet, and Ward all suggest that faithfulness to the antislavery cause means full resistance to slavery, and that such resistance, even as a Christian, does not preclude the possibility of violence. Walker sees the fight for freedom as a "heavenly cause." He affirms the need to resist tyrants and understands that violence may well be necessary for self-defense. Further, he contends that blacks have a *duty* to resist, even if it means death. Garnet echoes those sentiments when he tells the slave population that they have a responsibility to resist, and that it is better to die than to live as slaves. David Walker died just as the radical period of abolitionism was emerging. However, Pennington, Garnet, and Ward labored long enough in the abolitionist movement to experience moments of discouragement as the struggle to bring forth emancipation lingered on into decades. As resistance to slavery provoked a greater, more desperate defense of it from the South, with legislation and political circumstances seeming to lend greater support to maintaining it where it already flourished, Pennington, Garnet, and Ward became part of an increasingly more militant strain of abolitionism among blacks.

AMERICA'S RELIGIOUS AND POLITICAL HYPOCRISY

Consistent in all four authors is the theme of the religious and political hypocrisy of America in relation to this critical question of slavery. Each was familiar with the Declaration of Independence and how that document represented a political manifesto for a nation determined to project itself as a land of liberty with equal justice for all. The four freedom fighters express profound disappointment with America's failure to live up to those ideals and the seeming obtuseness of white Americans who fail to recognize the hypocrisy of proclaiming the value of liberty even as they hold others in bondage. Walker, who seems impressed with Thomas Jefferson as an intellectual statesman and author of the Declaration, exposes the errors in Jefferson's unconvincing attempts to reconcile the notion of liberty with slave-holding. The writings of Walker, Pennington, Garnet, and Ward indicate that they believed in the possibilities of the American experiment, and despite the long delay in black justice, they maintained the belief that one day white Americans would come to see their errors with regard to their treatment of blacks. However, none of the authors believed that repentance in America would come without agitation, challenge, and perhaps even violent conflict.

As much as they are disturbed by America's hypocrisy with regard to its political ideals, the four seem to have felt an even deeper righteous indignation toward the American church for its failure to live up to Christian principles with regard to how human beings are to relate to one another under God. Walker provides the strongest denunciation of the church of the four. However, the others also are keenly aware of the church's failings and, in particular, the failings of the clergy. Although each was as radical (if not more so) as William Lloyd Garrison in noting the corruption of the American church, few of them felt, as he did, that the church was so thoroughly corrupt as to be incapable of reform. This is a point that often separated black abolitionists from Garrison, even though they remained staunch supporters of his radical denunciation of slavery.

THE FIGHT FOR BLACK DIGNITY

We have seen some important areas of common ground among the four freedom fighters. However, the most significant point of commonality among the four rests with the notion that for black abolitionists, abolitionism was not simply a struggle to achieve the emancipation of enslaved blacks, as important as ending slavery was. A critical element in their understanding of abolitionism was the restoration of the full dignity of blacks. This concern for the human dignity of blacks suffused their antislavery work with a passion born of an existential urgency understandably lacking in those who did not share the fate of men and women of African descent. This acute sense of urgency was also the area in which black and white abolitionists probably differed the most, for it precluded political compromise, religious abstractions, and any acceptance of the notion that gradualism or open-ended patience was a warranted approach to achieve the goal of equal justice. Expressing this urgency, Walker wrote:

> It appears as though they are bent only on daring God Almighty to do his best—they chain and handcuff us and our children and drive us around the country like brutes, and

go into the house of the God of justice to return him thanks for having aided them in their infernal cruelties inflicted upon us. Will the Lord suffer this people to go on much longer, taking his holy name in vain? Will he not stop them, PREACHERS and all? O Americans! Americans! I call God–I call angels–I call men, to witness, that your DE-STRUCTION is *at hand,* and will be speedily consummated unless you REPENT.[1]

In Pennington's account of the degrading effects of slavery upon both slaves and masters, a decay that would prove worse for succeeding generations, it became clear that a swift breakdown of the institution of slavery was necessary to preserve the republic.[2] Ward, in summarizing the political implications of maintaining slavery, more explicitly pointed to the implications for the future of the republic: "The political issue is as deep, radical, and vital, in its kind: it involves the safety, stability, and not just the unity alone, but the very existence of the republic."[3] And Garnet, in addressing the slave population, noted their long suffering and exhorted them to spend no more time debating what the right course of action should be.[4]

In his critique of several Christian denominations, benevolent institutions, theological professors, and individual clergy with regard to their failure to challenge slavery and the resulting degradation of blacks in society, Samuel Ward identified what he thought was the crux of the matter, that is, contempt for black people.[5] Ward believed racial prejudice was at the heart of resistance to ending slavery and restoring the human dignity of blacks. His narrative addressed the issue of racial prejudice explicitly.

Garnet noted in his address to the slaves in 1843 that blacks were brought to America without their consent and were exposed to such treatment that it seemed "no cruelty [was] too great, no villainy and no robbery too abhorrent for even enlightened men to perform."[6] He notes that since their black ancestors arrived, succeeding generations have inherited their deeply degraded condition.[7] However, Garnet's intended audience is black slaves, who do not need a recitation of what it is like to be treated as brutes rather than persons for reasons tied directly to their blackness.

Pennington's narrative, which is directed toward a wider public, makes an explicit reference to the condition of blacks *as blacks;*

he notes the irony of the brutal, degrading institution of slavery being sustained by Christian slave holders. The language he uses explicitly demonstrates his outrage, which is directed against attempts to use Christianity to mitigate the sin of slavery and which points out the impact of racism upon the status of blacks:

> When Christians, and Christian ministers, then, talk about the "mildest form of slavery,"–"Christian masters," etc., I say my feelings are outraged. It is a great mistake to offer these as an extenuation of the system. It is calculated to mislead the public mind. The opinion seems to prevail, that the negro, after having toiled as a slave for centuries to enrich his white brother, to lay the foundation of his proud institutions, after having been sunk as low as slavery can sink him, needs now only a second-rate civilization, a lower standard of civil and religious privileges than the whites claim for themselves.[8]

WALKER'S ATTACK UPON RACISM

Walker's *Appeal* has several references to the issue of race as it pertains to blacks. In his discussion of the wretchedness of blacks because of slavery, he notes that other races and civilizations have been accorded recognition of their personhood but that that acknowledgment has been clearly denied to blacks in the Americas:

> MY BELOVED BRETHREN:–The Indians of North and of South America–the Greeks–the Irish, subjected under the king of Great Britain–the Jews, that ancient people of the Lord–the inhabitants of the islands of the sea–in fine, all the inhabitants of the earth, (except however, the sons of Africa) are called *men*, and of course are, and ought to be free. But we, (coloured people) and our children are *brutes*!! And of course are, and *ought to be* SLAVES to the American people and their children forever.[9]

Elsewhere Walker writes: "We are, in this generation, leveled by them [whites], almost on a level with the brute creation: and some of us they treat even worse than they do the brutes that perish. I only made this extract to show how much lower we are held, and how much more cruel we are treated by the Americans."[10]

In Walker's discussion he seeks to compare the plight of black American slaves to the plight of other enslaved populations during the course of history. In one section he compares the plight of the Hebrews under Egyptian slavery with that of blacks under slavery in a Christian nation. The issue of greatest concern for Walker at this point is the question of the humanity of the black slave. He observes:

> But to prove farther that the condition of the Israelites was better under the Egyptians than ours is under the whites, I call upon the professing Christians, I call upon the philanthropist, I call upon the very tyrant himself, to show me a page of history, either sacred or profane, on which a verse can be found, which maintains, that the Egyptians heaped the *insupportable insult* upon the children of Israel, by telling them that they were not of the *human family*. Can the whites deny this charge? Have they not, after having reduced us to the deplorable condition of slaves under their feet, held us up as descending originally from the tribes of *Monkeys* or *Orang-Outangs*? O! my God! I appeal to every man of feeling—is not this insupportable?[11]

Walker's style of punctuation and strategic capitalization of certain words and phrases clearly indicates his outrage as he reflects upon this state of affairs.

THE STAIN OF "NEGRO-HATE"

Ward's distress is no less apparent in his discussion of what he calls "Negro-hate." Ward devotes two small chapters to the problem of racism in the context of his account of his antislavery activities. As he defines what he means by antislavery labors, he notes that it includes "all the upright demeanour, gentlemanly bearing, Christian character, social progress, and material prosperity, of every coloured man, especially if he be a native of the United States."[12] Immediately, though, he notes that "the enemies of the Negro" deny the capacity of blacks for improvement or progress. Instead, they maintain that blacks are "deficient in morals, manners, intellect, and character." They maintain that "the Negro is neither fit for nor entitled to the rights, immunities and privileges, which the same parties say belong naturally to *all men*."[13] Ward, like Walker, alludes to the fact that some deny that blacks are even part of the human family, identifying two distinguished and learned persons in particular who have publicly made such a claim.[14] Ward singles out Americans for the distinction of being the cruelest to their enslaved and attributes this explicitly to Negro-hate. He views this Negro-hate or racism as universal.[15] Not only is racism a prevailing ideology of American thinking, it is pervasive in its practice.

In an earlier chapter Ward chronicles his personal experience of racism in the North, not as a slave, but as a free man in free territory (New York). Ward describes racism in this context as "ever-present" and "ever-crushing." The damage of such treatment on the psyche of one who seeks to improve oneself with the hope of being a productive member of society is incalculable.[16] And the experience of discrimination in the context of Christian worship—for example, not being allowed to receive communion until all white communicants had been served—was enough to drive some blacks out of the church permanently.[17]

PART III

THE ENEMY OF THE QUEST

Chapter 9

White Supremacy

The Scourge of American Society

Racism bloats and disfigures the face of the culture that practices it.
—Frantz Fanon, *Toward the African Revolution*

Historians now accept, to some degree or another, M. I. Finley's judgment that "the connection between slavery and racism has been a dialectical one, in which each element reinforced the other."[1] Before the 1830s, subordination of blacks was the practice of white Americans, and the inferiority of blacks was a common assumption, although it was rare for whites openly to assert the permanent inferiority of the black race.[2] Abolitionism would serve as the catalyst to unmask assertions of theoretical human equality and force practitioners of racial oppression to develop theories consonant with their racist behavior.[3] Dwight Dumond outlines several sociopolitical issues that intense intellectual debate had failed to resolve in the thirty years prior to the Civil War.[4] First, there was a debate over blacks' capacity for intellectual and moral improvement. Second, there was concern over the probable consequences of complete emancipation without the removal of blacks from the country. Third, there was discussion about the utility and character of the institution of slavery. Fourth, slavery's status under the U.S. Constitution was in dispute. Finally, concerns related to the nature of the federal government, the limits of its powers, and the residuary authority of the states were matters of intense discussion. Racial prejudice undergirded these debates, which were sustained among the intellectual and cultured classes by an uncritical, self-serving acceptance of the theory of biological inequality and racial inferiority of the black race.[5]

These sociopolitical issues were shaped by intellectual and pseudo-scientific developments during the period of modernity, which emerged in Europe and influenced America. In his extensive study on racism in the United States, sociologist Joe R. Feagin holds that "the new nation formed by European Americans in the late eighteenth century was openly and officially viewed as a white republic."[6] He maintains that the founding fathers sought to build a "racially based republic" in the face of monarchial opposition and against those people on the North American continent whom they defined as inferior.[7] In general, the founding fathers viewed those from Africa as slaves by *natural law*.[8] They reasoned that Africans were inferior beings who were fit by nature for enslavement by whites. However, as historian Don Fehrenbacher notes, a fully articulated theory of biological (and therefore permanent) black inferiority did not emerge until the second quarter of the nineteenth century.[9]

RACISM AND MODERNITY

Black religious philosopher Cornel West has done considerable work on the philosophical underpinnings of racism in the United States; his work is consistent with, though more philosophically elaborate than, Feagin's culturally based study of racism. As West notes, the Age of Enlightenment, from 1688 to 1789, witnessed the emergence of European modernity.[10] The basic features of early modern European culture were the increasing acceptance of the authority of science, the appearance of neo-classicism, and the subjectivist turn in philosophy.[11] The intellectual defense and institutional support of the practices of scientists became increasingly more persuasive to the literate population.[12]

West gives a brief account of the way in which the idea of white supremacy was constituted as an object of modern discourse in the West. He argues that the initial structure of modern discourse in the West actually "secretes" the idea of white supremacy. The authority of science, which was undergirded by a modern philosophical discourse guided by Greek ocular metaphors and Cartesian notions, promoted and encouraged the activities of observing, comparing, measuring, and ordering the physical characteristics of human bodies.[13] The recovery of classical antiquity in the modern West produced a "normative gaze," which is an ideal from which to order and compare observations. This ideal was drawn primarily from classical aesthetic values of beauty, proportion, and human form, and classical cultural standards of moderation, self-control, and harmony.[14] The fusion of scientific investigation, Cartesian epistemology, and classical ideals produced forms of rationality, scientific methodology, and notions of objectivity that precluded black equality in beauty, culture, and intellectual capacity.[15] West argues that the role of classical aesthetic and cultural norms in the emergence of the idea of white supremacy cannot be overestimated. In fact, these norms were consciously projected and promoted by many influential Enlightenment writers, artists, and scholars. West contends that what is distinctive about classical aesthetic and cultural norms of modernity is that they provided an acceptable authority for the idea of white supremacy. This legitimization was closely linked with the major authority on truth and knowledge in the modern world, namely, the institution of science.[16]

A second stage of the emergence of the idea of white supremacy as an object of modern discourse occurred in the rise of phrenology (the reading of skulls) and physiognomy (the reading of faces).[17] These new disciplines, which were closely connected with anthropology, served as an open platform for the propagation of the idea of white supremacy because these disciplines acknowledged the European value-laden character of their observations, which was based on classical aesthetic and cultural ideals. West maintains that the intellectual legitimacy of the idea of white supremacy, though grounded in marginal disciplines, was pervasive. This legitimacy can be seen by the extent to which racism permeated the writings of the major figures of the Enlightenment: Montesquieu, Voltaire, Hume, Thomas Jefferson, and Immanuel Kant. West provides documentation from their writings to support his case. Given the direction of modern discourse, West concludes, the emergence of the idea of white supremacy "seem[ed] inevitable."[18]

Inevitable or not, before the end of the nineteenth century a constellation of religious, historical, and biological theories positing the inferiority of persons of African descent was embraced as time-honored truth by white Americans.[19] Racist ideology provided a rationalization for the marginal position given to free blacks in the North and for the enslavement of blacks in the South.[20] As abolitionists began to challenge the institution more aggressively after the 1830s, theories of biological inequality and racial inferiority of the black race were adopted by proslavery factions in order to justify slavery. One example of the nature of proslavery thought can be seen in an essay by Thomas R. Dew, a professor at William and Mary College, who represented the proslavery faction. In this essay Dew set forth a more thorough and comprehensive justification of the institution by challenging proponents of gradual emancipation and colonization in Western Virginia. He sought to demonstrate that colonization was an impossible scheme because the increase of the black population would exceed the number of blacks that could be colonized.

Dew justified slavery on several grounds.[21] First, servitude had been a necessary state of human progress and therefore could not be regarded as evil in itself. Second, the concrete circumstances of Southern life *required* slavery, and no set of "abstract" principles of liberty could obscure the basic "fact" that blacks were not prepared for freedom.[22]

Dew also discussed black character and prospects, maintaining a view that at times coincided with a "traditional quasi-environmentalist assumption" about the nature of most racial differences.[23] He viewed blacks as having the "habits and feelings" of slaves, whites those of masters. Yet Dew did not believe that if blacks were freed they would lose their sense of degradation. He maintained that certain habits had been formed that legislation could not alter; nor would being free change the prejudices of whites against them.

RACISM AND THE DEFENSE OF SLAVERY

By the 1830s slavery had shifted in the eyes of its supporters from a "necessary evil" to "a positive good," as abolitionists argued for the inherent sinfulness of slavery.[24] The South would further clarify its racial views and come to assert as a major part of its case the unambiguous concept of inherent black inferiority, as abolitionists contended that racial equality was something to be achieved *in the United States* and not through colonization.[25] Historian George M. Fredrickson maintains that South Carolina led the way in this kind of Southern thinking, which can be seen in a speech Governor George McDuffie made to the South Carolina General Assembly in 1835. In that speech McDuffie told the Assembly that blacks were "destined by providence" for slavery and that this was evident not only in their skin color but also in "the intellectual inferiority and natural improvidence of this race." Further, McDuffie maintained that blacks were "unfit for self-government of any kind" and that "in all respects, physical, moral, and political, they were inferior to millions of the human race."[26]

In time, this view of inherent permanent inequality, which grounded the concept of slavery as a positive good, became a rationale not only for slavery itself but also for post-emancipation forms of racial oppression.[27] The attitudes that underlay the belief that blacks were doomed by nature itself to perpetual servitude and subordination to whites were not new. However, when they assumed the status of a dogmatic assertion, and were held with an aura of philosophical authority by leading southern spokesmen and their northern supporters in the 1830s, the notion of the inherent, permanent inequality of the race became for the first time the basis of a world view.[28] Inherent, permanent inequality became "an explicit ideology around which the beneficiaries of white supremacy would organize themselves and their thoughts."[29]

On the one hand, colonizationists seemed to have stimulated an indirect and pragmatic defense of slavery as a regional necessity, but their occasional expressions of a theoretical racial egalitarianism had not forced their Southern opponents to proclaim vigorously that blacks were inherently inferior and slavish. Because proponents of colonization had not challenged the necessity or inevitability of black subservience as a fact of life in the United States, Southerners felt less threatened by colonization. On the other hand, the claim of radical abolitionists that Christianity and the Declaration of Independence not only affirmed equality in theory but cried out for its immediate implementation forced the defenders of black subordination to launch a dogmatic defense. Because the agitation of abolitionism threatened the social order, elaborate claims became more of a necessity.[30]

Fredrickson has identified a number of arguments that proslavery theorists used in the 1830s and 1840s for black inferiority. These theorists emphasized the historical case against the black man based on his supposed failure to develop a "civilized" way of life in Africa.[31] Africans were viewed as engaging in "unmitigated savagery, cannibalism, devil worship, and licentiousness."[32] Another argument, which constituted an early form of the biological argument, was based on real or imagined physiological anatomical differences, especially in terms of cranial characteristics and facial angles, which were viewed as "explaining" the mental and physical inferiority of blacks. There was also the appeal to fear among whites of widespread miscegenation, which has often reached hysterical proportions historically.[33] Proslavery opponents feared that the abolition of slavery would lead to intermarriage and the degeneracy of the white race. Although these fears had been present earlier in a nascent form, the arguments behind them were brought together swiftly and organized in a strict pattern once defenders of slavery found themselves in a propaganda war with the abolitionists.[34]

Fredrickson maintains that as part of an effort to gain widespread support for their views, proslavery polemicists turned their attention to the free blacks of the North to help buttress their arguments.[35] This was not a difficult ploy for proslavery polemicists to enact, because the wave of Revolutionary era egalitarianism that had led the Northern states to abolish slavery was "all but gone" by the 1830s.[36] White Northerners shared their Southern counterparts' conviction that blacks were a grossly inferior race that could never hope to interact with whites on equal terms.[37] In fact, a northern majority would respond to the abolitionist movement of the 1830s with bitter hostility.[38]

In the wake of emancipation Northern blacks found persecution and exclusion. They were disenfranchised in all but a few Northern states. They were not permitted to bear arms in state militias. They were precluded from testifying against whites in court. They were viewed not as contributing members of society but as barely tolerable "nuisances." Public services, including schools, were not always available to them. And there were a host of local ordinances, varying from place to place, that restricted where blacks could live, work, travel, and even gather in public.[39] With such obstacles to productive living, they were presented not as a population degraded by white prejudice but as examples of their *natural* unfitness for freedom.

As the debates continued, there were some who posed the question of how to treat a race that is perceived as inferior. For example, Owen Lovejoy, an abolitionist Congressman from Illinois, and the brother of martyred editor Elijah Lovejoy, asserted that even if blacks were an inferior race, there still was no right to enslave them.[40] Lovejoy maintained that to do so would place the weak everywhere at the mercy of the strong; it would place the poor at the mercy of the rich; and those who were intellectually deficient at the mercy of those gifted in mental endowment.[41] Southerners countered this argument with the claim that blacks were "ideally suited to slavery; that blacks found happiness and fulfillment only when they had a white master."[42] Yet, these same Southerners were secretly fearful of the insurrections that belied this view of blacks as being especially suited for slavery. Such Southerners argued that free blacks and abolitionists put notions into the heads of enslaved blacks that really ran counter to their natural affinities. These proslavery advocates maintained that far from being degraded by the institution, blacks in slavery were better off than they would have been in Africa.[43]

Other proponents of slavery theorized that blacks were by nature savages and brutes, and that under slavery they were domesticated or to a limited degree "civilized." Under this theory, docility was not natural to blacks but was an artificial result of slavery. The control of the master needed to be firm and assured; then the slaves would be happy, loyal, and affectionate. However, if the master's authority was removed or weak, the slaves would revert to blood-thirsty savagery.[44] As proof of this, whites pointed to Haiti, the British West Indies, and Liberia, as examples of places where the domesticating influence of slavery had been removed and blacks had reverted to barbarism.[45] The views that bestial savagery constituted the basic black character and that the loyal "Sambo" figure was a social product of slavery helped to channel genuine fears and anxieties by suggesting a program for preventive action. A slave could be lovable, but a free black would be a monster.[46]

Some Southerners believed that it was more difficult to mistreat blacks or overwork blacks than whites. Others even concluded that, for the most part, a master need not concern himself with the possibility that blacks had normal human sensibilities. The alleged animal insensitivity of blacks was also invoked as a basis for denying the presence of familial affection among slaves, thereby implicitly justifying the breakup of families.[47] Fredrickson argues that the South's fundamental conception of itself as a slaveholding society was unstable. (I would add, also contradictory and illogical.) On the one hand, the notion of the slave as dependent or childlike implied one kind of social order (paternalism, perhaps). On the other hand, the view that blacks were essentially subhuman suggested another social order (the kind of brutality found on some plantations).[48]

One thing that emerges from Fredrickson's discussion is the inconsistent world view of the nature of black inequality and the nature of the basic character of blacks in general. Blinded by notions of white supremacy, whites could not conjure up a consistent portrait of blacks that would justify their enslavement. One faction emphasized black docility, another black brutality. However, in the North as well as the South, there was a commitment to white supremacy that makes it difficult to make a qualitative differentiation between the two areas on the issue of racism from the perspective of the experiences of blacks, North or South, free or enslaved. In many ways the essential Christian belief that equality resides in the eyes of God was often not seen as an impediment to a hierarchical order in human relations between the races.[49]

THE FACES OF RACISM IN THE NORTH AND SOUTH

If whites in the North and South held similar views about the inferiority of blacks, what accounts for the difference in their position on slavery? Apart from the fact that slavery was economically profitable in the South in a way that it never was in the North, one can make distinctions about the kind of racism present in the two sections of the country. In *White Supremacy*, George M. Fredrickson appropriates the work of psycho-historian Joel Kovel, who attempts to explain the difference between the North and the South in terms of racism. Kovel maintains that there are two forms of racism operative: "dominative" and "aversive." Dominative racism was found in the South, where the domination of blacks became the cornerstone of society. When racists felt threatened by the presence of blacks, they resorted to direct violence. The South believed that it needed blacks as a servile labor force and social "mudsill" (permanent menial class), and Southerners developed elaborate rationalizations for keeping blacks in that position.[50] Aversive racism was found in the North, where blacks found themselves out of place. When threatened by the presence of blacks, the aversive white Northerners turned away from social interaction and created barriers to keep themselves from close contact with blacks. Kovel notes that the North revealed its basic attitudes in laws that excluded black migrants from entering individual states. They also engaged a flood of theorizing, particularly in the 1850s, that advocated the expatriation or natural extinction of blacks.[51]

Kovel's categorizations of racism in the context of the intersectional strife between the North and the South are useful. But, as Fredrickson points out, one must keep in mind that the crucial difference between the sections with regard to racism lies in the prominence of the racial attitudes in each area. The dominative racism was a much more significant component of the Southern world view than aversive racism was of the Northern. In some ways Northerners were able to subordinate their racial sensibilities to their consideration of the imperatives of nationalism. However, in the South it was necessary to translate all social and political values into racial terms, for it was not just slavery in general but black slavery in particular that was the keystone of Southern social and economic order.[52]

During the 1840s and 1850s, just as inter-sectional strife began to increase, the conclusions of scientists on the nature and extent of racial diversity came to play an important role in the discussion of black servitude for the first time.[53] In educated circles in both South and North there was growing belief that Thomas Jefferson had been correct in anticipating that science would eventually decide conclusively whether blacks were biologically equal to whites. By now a "substantial segment" of Northern opinion was prepared to embrace the biological theory that blacks belonged to a separate and inferior species.[54] In the South, susceptibility to extreme racist thinking was reinforced in some ways by the rise of democratic and egalitarian aspirations among whites. Jacksonian democracy carried the rhetoric of popular democracy to an extreme almost unparalleled in American political history. But it also condoned a form of anti-black demagoguery that anticipated the Southern race baiters of a later era. As Fredrickson observes, even the most radical spokesman for "the common man," including those associated with working men's movements, went out of their way to emphasize that their "democracy" was for whites only.[55]

EQUALITY FOR *SOME*

According to Fredrickson, the conjunction of white egalitarianism and black proscription against full participation in a democratic society was more than mere rhetoric. This conjunction was put into practice in New York in 1821 and in Pennsylvania in 1838. In these states constitutional extensions of white suffrage were accompanied by restrictions or (in the case of Pennsylvania) complete denial of blacks' right to vote. By the 1850s an established relationship in the North between democratic ideology and extreme racism was in evidence.[56] Arguments that served to exclude blacks from the community of equals defined by the Declaration of Independence were now welcomed by many who claimed to be in the vanguard of the movement to implement the Declaration's egalitarian philosophy.[57] Two years after the Dred Scott case, which denied American citizenship to all blacks, Abraham Lincoln observed that some Northern Democrats were now asserting openly that when the Declaration of Independence spoke of "all men," this did *not* include blacks. Eventually there would be some who would demonstrate in detail how science had now laid a firm foundation for the ideological marriage of interracial egalitarianism and overt Negrophobia that had long been popular among Northern Democrats.[58]

This issue of the white desire for homogeneity seems to have occurred to George Fredrickson as he reflected upon unfolding events. He raises the possible objection that slave holders and other Americans who exploit blacks economically or socially have no desire to get rid of the black population.[59] He goes on to say that in the nineteenth-century South the presence of an egalitarian ethos seemed to require that blacks be regarded not merely as aliens, but as creatures not quite human. However, my read of the material suggests that if it were possible, white Americans would have eliminated blacks from the American experiment.

Fredrickson observes that with the development in the 1840s and 1850s of scientific race theory and a new sense of Caucasian or Anglo-Saxon racial pride, it became possible to articulate a concern for continued "homogeneity" with more authority. However, the "pseudo-homogeneity" that could be attained by the exclusion of blacks from the community of citizens through enslavement, patterns of discrimination, and ultimately through the absolute prohibition of intermarriage did not satisfy all segments of anti-black opinion in the pre–Civil War period. Some "aberrant" Southerners objected openly to the physical presence of blacks, however lowly and subordinate they might be, and even advocated deportation of the entire race. However, such an attitude was much more common in the North, because Northerners lacked direct dependence on black labor and consequently tended to look upon free blacks as a superfluous population.[60]

In actuality, black exclusionist sentiments were particularly strong in the Midwest, where there were various efforts in the 1840s and 1850s to prevent black immigration and to remove blacks who were already there. Indiana prohibited all blacks from entering the state in 1851; Illinois followed suit in 1853.[61] The Midwest saw an upsurge of the kind of colonizationist activity that was openly and explicitly concerned with simply getting rid of the local free blacks by sending them anywhere outside the United States.[62] Many in the Midwest were fearful of receiving an overflow of the black population from the South. Some went so far as to advocate either deportation of blacks altogether or the migration of the entire black population to the South. Fredrickson notes that this fear of "black peril" reached "panic proportions" when the Civil War brought the prospect of emancipation. This was actually the kind of fear that gripped proponents of colonization since the late eighteenth century. However, what was new in this fear was that the 1840s and 1850s brought greater impetus to the hope for homogenization through the removal or elimination of the black.[63]

RACISM AND SECTIONAL CONFLICTS

Fredrickson maintains that there were larger political developments that must be considered in order to explain why speculation about denying blacks a continued existence in the United States was so frequently ventured and so widely accepted in the North while sectional conflict climaxed with the prospect of black emancipation.[64] First, there was the rise of a new sense of American nationalism that had racial overtones. This tendency to identify race and nationality was present in the public debate that took place between 1846 and 1848 on the question of whether the United States should follow up its victory in the Mexican War by annexing all of Mexico. There were those who feared the annexation of Mexico because the Mexican population was largely of Indian or mixed blood. They believed that American interests would be well served only if acquisition were limited to thinly populated areas contiguous to the United States.[65] This debate had clear implications for blacks, reinforcing racial limitations on the kind of people who could be incorporated into the country.[66]

Another issue was the controversy over the future of slavery in the territories, a struggle that began in 1846 with the effort in Congress to enact the Wilmot Proviso. This measure prohibited slavery in all areas acquired in the Mexican War. This political conflict had been temporarily dampened by the Compromise of 1850; however, it resurfaced anew with the Kansas-Nebraska Act of 1854. It would increase in intensity until the presidential election of Abraham Lincoln in 1860 and the secession of the South in 1861. This was primarily a struggle over what kind of institutions—slave or free—would triumph in the western territories and ultimately in the nation as a whole. In the North it was also viewed as a contest to decide whether white or black populations would predominate in the new areas.[67]

Whether black slaves or free white men were destined in the long run to provide the labor for the existing territories, the climatic racialist theory of nationality seemed to provide a clear, unequivocal answer.[68] (The climatic theory posited that blacks were not suited constitutionally to this climate, that the warmer climates were a natural habitat for blacks.) The late antebellum period saw Southern leaders make an issue of the status of slavery in areas that they themselves often acknowledged were unpromising as plantation regions.[69] Southerners were drawn into a contest for the control of regions that the North had come to regard as set aside by nature for the white man and for free labor as a way of ensuring that there was sufficient balance between the slave and free states to ensure the preservation of slavery in the South.[70] Fredrickson asserts that "the political free-soil movement, which developed out of Northern anxieties about Southern expansionism and the extension of slavery, combined principled opposition to slavery as an institution with a considerable amount of antipathy to the presence of Negroes on any basis whatever."[71]

Those in the free-soil movement did not feel that blacks had a future life in the North, unless they were artificially introduced as slaves. However, members of the movement could not agree on what in the long run should happen to blacks in the South. There were many who opposed slavery as practiced in the South in principle but were convinced, nevertheless, that blacks were unfit to associate with whites and could never be granted civil equality. After the outbreak of the Civil War, some Northerners were willing to concede a slice of the United States for exclusive black occupancy because they became convinced that emancipation would lead naturally to such a result and might even narrow the existing zone of the black population.[72]

Fredrickson argues that predictions that the containment and eventual disappearance of slavery would bring about a welcome division of the United States into a vast white region and a severely restricted "African belt" were not the ultimate expressions of Northern racial nationalism. He states that the full white nationalist position, which was the logical outcome of the desire for racial and institutional homogeneity, was more radical. It really pointed toward the elimination of blacks as an element in the population, either through planned colonization, unplanned migration, or their extermination from "natural" processes. The new climatic racial determinism, he states, was one factor in reviving interest in various emigration and colonization schemes for blacks during the 1850s.[73]

Fredrickson observes that the belief that the American race problem could be solved by establishing black colonies in Central America or the Caribbean (due to the racial climatic theories) did not end with the outbreak of the Civil War and the expectation of slavery's demise. Instead, it was advocated with new urgency as a requisite part of the emancipation process by Abraham Lincoln and other leading Republicans who wanted to counter the charge that the party was pro-black.[74]

WHITE SUPREMACY: A PERVASIVE PHENOMENON

In reflecting upon the degree to which the idea of white supremacy was pervasive, Historian Mia Bay maintains that in the first half of the century, racist ideology provided a rationalization for the enslavement of African Americans in the South and for the marginal position accorded to free blacks in the North. After the Civil War this ideology reached new heights in a society where racial proscription continued to govern the social and economic relations between white and black people.[75]

Economists Robert William Fogel and Stanley L. Engerman conclude, and I concur, that the belief in black incompetence was given a powerful stimulus by the racial theories that came into prominence during the first half of the nineteenth century. These theories, which asserted that blacks and whites were of different species or at least that blacks were an "inferior variety" of the human species, were embraced by Northerners as well as Southerners, by critics of slavery as well as its defenders. The African origins of blacks were thought to have contributed to biological "defects." While some attributed racial differences to geographic factors, others saw the "backwardness" of blacks as rooted in their "savage" ancestry. Regardless of the cause, the supposed innate inferiority of the black race was said to manifest itself in laziness, limited intellectual capacity, childlike simplicity, docility, sensuousness, and tempestuousness. Fogel and Engerman contend that it is important to stress that these racist views were not embraced merely in popular thought. They were the reigning tenets of mid-nineteenth-century anthropology in Europe as well as in the United States.[76]

We can conclude from this discussion that racial considerations played a significant role in shaping and intensifying inter-sectional conflict. As Fredrickson notes, although very few white Americans actually endorsed the principle of racial equality on the eve of the Civil War, there were significant differences of opinion regarding the question of what racial differences meant for the future of American society.[77] We can also say that even though the North and South differed in their attitudes toward the necessity for slavery, both the North and the South agreed that blacks were inferior and many from both regions doubted that they could ever be absorbed into American society on the basis of any kind of equality.[78]

A BLACK ABOLITIONIST PERSPECTIVE

If racial prejudice prompted debate among the white intellectual elite of the nineteenth century, racial prejudice and its impact upon blacks were topics that black abolitionists often addressed within the context of their antislavery speeches and writings. Their discourse and reflection tended toward the concrete and personal rather than the theoretical and social. A brief survey of views of some prominent black abolitionists on their experience of racial prejudice as an assault on their human dignity follows.

The Fortens

James Forten, patriarch of the black abolitionist Forten family of Philadelphia, responded in February 1813 to an effort by a number of white Pennsylvanians who petitioned the state legislature for measures that included the requirement that all blacks register with the state; that a special tax be levied on free blacks for the support of their poor; and the requirement that any black coming into Pennsylvania be registered within twenty-four hours or face fine, imprisonment, and possible sale.[79] Particularly disturbed by the possibility that some legislators did not view blacks as people, Forten wrote:

> Why are we not to be considered as men? Has the God who made the white man and the black left any record declaring us a different species? Are we not sustained by the same power, supported by the same food, hurt by the same wounds, wounded by the same wrongs, pleased with the same delights, and propagated by the same means? And

should we not then enjoy the same liberty, and be protected by the same laws?[80]

Forty-two years later, Forten's seventeen-year-old granddaughter, Charlotte Forten, a budding antislavery activist, records her experiences with racial prejudice in Salem, Massachusetts, in her journal:

> I wonder that every colored person is not a misanthrope. Surely we have everything to make us hate mankind. I have met girls in the schoolroom—they have been thoroughly kind and cordial to me—perhaps the next day met them in the street—they feared to recognize me; these I can but regard now with scorn and contempt.[81]

Charlotte Forten concedes that such experiences of prejudice are "trifles" in comparison with greater public wrongs that some have to endure, but, she maintains, these "apparent trifles" are difficult to endure and teach one to meet others with suspicion and distrust.[82] She continues to wrestle with the impact of such experiences on one's ability to respond in Christian love:

> Oh! It is hard to go through life meeting contempt with contempt, hatred with hatred, fearing, with too good reason to love and trust hardly any one whose skin is white. . . . In the bitter, passionate feeling of my soul again and again there rises the quest "When, oh! When shall this cease?" "Is there no help?" "How long oh! How long must we continue to suffer—to endure?"[83]

After a cry of despair, she suggests the means by which her people may overcome the burden of racial prejudice:

> Conscience answers it is wrong, it is ignoble to despair; let us labor earnestly and faithfully to acquire knowledge, to break down the barriers of prejudice and oppression. Let us take courage, never ceasing to work,—hoping and believing that if not for us, for another generation there is a better, brighter day in store, when slavery and prejudice shall

vanish before the glorious light of Liberty and Truth; when the rights of every colored man shall everywhere be acknowledged and respected, and he shall be treated as a man and a brother.[84]

Charlotte Forten's answer to the problem of racial prejudice against blacks is similar to that of Walker, Pennington, Garnet, and Ward. She places great store on the acquisition of knowledge as a way of mitigating the effects of the degradation that afflicts not only enslaved black persons but free people as well.

Charlotte Forten's paternal aunt, Sarah L. Forten, also an antislavery activist, once responded in writing in April 1837 to a request by white abolitionist Angelina Grimke Weld to tell her of the effect prejudice had had on her life. In part, Sarah Forten responded:

> In reply to your question—of the "effect of Prejudice" on myself, I must acknowledge that it has often embittered my feelings, particularly when I recollect that we are the innocent victims of it for you are well aware that it originates from dislike to the color of the skin, as much as from the degradation of Slavery. I am peculiarly sensitive on this point, and consequently seek to avoid as much as possible mingling with those who exist under its influence.[85]

Undoubtedly, Sarah Forten's strategy to avoid the discomfiture of racial prejudice, particularly in the public domain, was widely practiced by other African Americans.

Clarissa C. Lawrence

In 1838 the Salem (Massachusetts) Female Anti Slavery Society prepared a resolution against racism, which was written in response to the burning of the newly constructed Pennsylvania Hall in Philadelphia, where antislavery activists had gathered for a convention. A mob of anti-abolitionists had set the hall on fire because of "an audience promiscuously mixed up of blacks and whites, sitting together in amalgamated ease."[86] Scholar Dorothy Sterling notes that black women did not often take the floor at such conventions; however, black antislavery activist Clarissa C. Lawrence was moved to respond to the Salem Anti-Slavery Society's resolution on racism:

> We meet the monster prejudice *everywhere*. We have not power to contend with it, we are so down-trodden. . . . We want light; we ask it, and it is denied us. Why are we thus treated? Prejudice is the cause. It kills its thousands every day; it follows us everywhere, even to the grave; but, blessed be God! *It* stops there. You must pray it down. Faith and prayer will do wonders in the anti-slavery cause. Place yourselves, dear friends, in our stead. We are blamed for not filling useful places in society; but give us light, give us learning, and see then what places we can occupy.[87]

Maria W. Stewart

Maria W. Stewart, black abolitionist and acquaintance of David Walker, knew well the prejudice that Clarissa Lawrence said "kills its thousands every day." Stewart notes in an address delivered to abolitionists in Boston in 1833:

> African rights and liberty is a subject that ought to fire the breast of every free man of color in these United States, and excite in his bosom a lively, deep, decided, and heart-felt interest. When I cast my eyes on the long list of illustrious names that are enrolled on the bright annals of fame among the whites, I turn my eyes within and ask my thoughts, "Where are the names of *our* illustrious ones?"[88]

Stewart also notes the condition of degradation in which blacks have allowed themselves to be placed and expresses her outrage:

> We have been imposed upon, insulted, and derided on every side; and now, if we complain, it is considered as the height of impertinence. We have suffered ourselves to be considered as dastards, cowards, mean, faint-hearted wretches; and on this account . . . many despise us, and would gladly spurn us from their presence. . . . These things

have fired my soul with a holy indignation and compelled
me thus to come forward and endeavor to turn their attention to knowledge and improvement, for knowledge is
power.[89]

Although Stewart concedes that she is "sensible of former prejudices," she maintains that it is high time that such prejudices and
animosities come to an end.[90] Her remedy is a combination of
prophetic witness, in keeping with the spirit of Walker, Garnet,
Pennington, and Ward, and a heavy dose of active self-develop-
ment on the part of blacks. For example, Stewart writes, "We this
day are considered as one of the most degraded races upon the
face of the earth. It is useless for us any longer to sit with our hands
folded reproaching the whites, for that will never elevate us."[91]

She implores black men, and especially black youth, to avoid
spending time on frivolous activities that waste their time, money,
and other resources. Instead, they should set themselves on a path
of self-improvement, giving attention to matters of faith in order
to counteract the degradation of black life in racist America.[92]

Frederick Douglass

Frederick Douglass echoes Stewart's message of uplift but suggests that the answer to the degradation that faces both enslaved
and free blacks lies in assuming a broader class of employment
opportunities rather than sticking solely to the menial jobs that
have become associated with their degraded status.[93] Like
Pennington, Garnet, and Ward, Douglass had been a fugitive slave,
originally from Maryland. His experiences of slavery had left their
mark. He had lived under several masters, some benign and others cruel. His experiences as a field slave for a particularly malicious slave owner led to two defining moments for Douglass. One
was the breaking of his "body, soul, and spirit," in which he sensed
in himself that he had been transformed from a man into a brute.
In his autobiographical slave narrative Douglass writes, "My natural elasticity was crushed, my intellect languished, the disposition
to read departed, the cheerful spark that lingered about my eye
died; the dark night of slavery closed in upon me; and behold a
man transformed into a brute!"[94]

The second defining moment came after a confrontation with this same master. Douglass describes it as follows:

> This battle with Mr. Covey was the turning-point in my career as a slave. It rekindled the few expiring embers of freedom, and revived within me a sense of my own manhood. It recalled the departed self-confidence, and inspired me again with a determination to be free. . . . I felt as I never felt before. It was a glorious resurrection, from the tomb of slavery, to the heaven of freedom. My long-crushed spirit rose, cowardice departed, bold defiance took its place; and I now resolved that, however long I might remain a slave in form, the day had passed forever when I could be a slave in fact. I did not hesitate to let it be known of me, that the white man who expected to succeed in whipping, must also succeed in killing me.[95]

This steely resolve served Douglass well in the course of his flight to freedom.

Douglass also gained another insight about himself as he reflected upon the psychology of enslavement:

> I have observed this in my experience of slavery,—that whenever my condition was improved, instead of its increasing my contentment, it only increased my desire to be free, and set me to thinking of plans to gain my freedom. I have found that, to make a contented slave, it is necessary to make a thoughtless one. It is necessary to darken his moral and mental vision, and, as far as possible, to annihilate the power of reason. He must be able to detect no inconsistencies in slavery; he must be made to feel that slavery is right; and he can be brought to that only when he ceases to be a man.[96]

Douglass experienced within his own soul the descent into dehumanization, which included his time as a slave and then as a fugitive, and this personal experience confirmed his sense of solidarity with the enslaved. Noting the "grievous wrongs" that black people have experienced, Douglass says in his 1848 address to the black people of the United States, that they have been burdened by a doctrine "perseveringly proclaimed in high places in church and state, that it is impossible for colored men to rise from ignorance and debasement, to intelligence and respectability" and that this "doctrine" has made a deep impression on the public mind in general and it has also had an effect upon blacks.[97]

Although this "doctrine" is due to prejudice, Douglass affirms the appropriateness of maintaining hope, and he encourages blacks to cooperate with those whites and their institutions that are dedicated to the abolition of slavery. One important way to counteract the pervasiveness of racial prejudice is to refute the underlying assumptions through engagement in the kind of work that belies the incapability of blacks to progress and take their rightful place in society. Accordingly, he writes:

> Every blow of the sledge hammer, wielded by a sable arm, is a powerful blow in support of our cause. Every colored mechanic, is by virtue of circumstances, an elevator of his race. Every house built by black men, is a strong tower against the allied hosts of prejudice. It is impossible for us to attach too much importance to this aspect of the subject.[98]

Thus, Douglass bears witness to blacks' struggle with the dehumanizing racial prejudice rampant in American society.

Chapter 10

The Specter of Racism
Infects Abolitionism

*[Charles Sumner] . . . prided himself . . . on the image he had of
himself as a crusader for the rights of Negroes—though people said
he never spoke with or became a friend of any individual Negro.*
—Dorothy Meserve Kunhardt and Philip B. Kunhardt Jr.,
Twenty Days

There is a bit of irony, if not humor, as one reflects upon this
epigraph, which offers a twofold picture of Charles Sumner. Lincoln historians Dorothy Meserve Kunhardt and Philip B. Kunhardt
Jr. describe Sumner as "a passionate, impatient abolitionist" who
was a thorn in the side of President Lincoln during the Civil War,
pushing the president relentlessly to emancipate the slaves, while
Lincoln brooded over the preservation of the Union.[1] The epigraph lends a degree of credibility to the frequent complaint of
blacks that they often found their white counterparts in the abolitionist movement inclined to abstraction over matters related to
emancipation.[2] Some might have seen themselves as mightily cru-
sading for *the black,* but the personal aspect of the conflict over
slavery, the individual black *person* oppressed under the system
was far removed from the experience of the white crusader. This
was certainly not true of all white abolitionists. For example, William Lloyd Garrison maintained a close friendship with the black
Forten family, as did the abolitionist poet John Greenleaf Whittier.

Also, the Grimke sisters, Sarah and Angelina, maintained friendships with members of the Forten family and other blacks they encountered in the movement. Nevertheless, white abolitionists along the continuum of various classification systems were not immune to the specter of racism in American society.

Support for emancipation of the slaves did not *necessarily* imply equality of blacks with whites. To make this assertion does not denigrate the importance of the role of whites in the abolitionist movement. It simply highlights the reality that whites did not perceive a necessary equation of the two concepts, whereas for blacks, the equation was self-evident. Although there were differences in perspectives and approaches between black and white abolitionists, the equation of black emancipation with a corresponding restoration of black dignity was probably the single most important issue that distinguished black abolitionism from its white counterpart. It is not that blacks believed that freeing the slaves would automatically bring a corresponding emancipation from white supremacy, but rather that, for blacks, restoration of their dignity was just as important, if not more so, than simply relieving them from uncompensated labor. The battle for their inclusion into the human family against the prevailing ethos of white supremacy provided the existential urgency that fueled black abolitionists in a way that their white counterparts could not experience. This is particularly true because even white abolitionist crusaders were subject to racial prejudice, which hindered them from being as persistent in leading the charge toward racial equality as they might otherwise have been. The specter of racism, even in the ranks of the abolitionists, helps to explain why the black abolitionists' quest for human dignity remained unfulfilled after emancipation.

Scholars have identified a number of issues that had a negative impact upon the degree to which the abolitionist movement could be understood as genuinely interracial. Some of those differences had to do with insensitivity to the degree of suffering blacks experienced under the system. Some differences reflected differing perceptions about what freedom meant. However, the largest difference between whites and blacks involved in abolitionism stemmed from blindness on the part of whites about their own susceptibility to the web of white supremacy. Even among the more "enlightened" and racially sensitive whites, a degree of paternalism often impeded their ability to work alongside blacks on a basis of equality.

THE CONCILIATORY APPROACH OF QUAKERS

As previously noted, the Quakers were among the earliest abolitionists and were attentive to antislavery measures prior to the 1830s, though it should be noted that they were never a large slave-holding group to begin with. They had a strong theological basis for their objection to slavery. George Fox, one of their most prominent leaders, warned against the danger inherent in the master-slave relationship as early as 1657, when he observed the practice of slavery in the West Indies. Fox preached against slavery and taught that Christ had died for blacks as well as whites. Fox asserted the brotherhood of men through the sacrifice of Christ, and from there reasoned that the servitude of blacks should end in freedom, just as it did for whites.[3] Fox's teaching had a great deal of influence upon later Quaker prophets such as George Keith. Keith was outspoken against slavery and took his cue from the writings of Fox, arguing that Christ had died for all, that Christians in general and Quakers in particular should do all in their power to free slaves from bondage.[4] Keith maintained that since slavery violated the Golden Rule, Christians ought to assist runaway slaves to escape.[5]

Despite the strong theological background for opposition to slavery, the Quakers' tactic of mild discouragement of the slave trade rendered their efforts at emancipation rather tepid. Quakers, such as John Woolman, who had a religious orientation in their antislavery efforts, tended to be moderates whose approach was conciliatory toward slave holders, even as they condemned the practice of slavery. They also favored colonization. Early Quaker abolitionists were gradualists who thought that an abhorrence of the institution would work its way among others. They trusted that a slow but inevitable operation of religious and egalitarian principles would bring the practice of slavery to an end. It was the duty of society to wait for that process to run its course. Because they believed that slavery would gradually die out, they expected blacks to bear up patiently until the death of slavery at some distant, unspecified date. Their word to free blacks was to live within their means so that they could share their resources with the less fortunate. Free blacks were also expected to cultivate feelings of gratitude to God for the blessings they had received.[6] Free blacks who encountered slaves were expected to exhort them to be content with their situation, so that their masters would respond with "humanity and gentleness."[7]

These early abolitionists took a conciliatory approach toward offending members of the community who had not yet refrained from slave-holding. Their posture was reflective of their commitment to peaceful ways of addressing conflict, and they viewed opposition to slave holders as opposition to a brother, not an enemy.[8] They sought to impress upon their Southern brethren that they did not wish to interfere with the rights of property, and to that end, supported compensation to slave owners with emancipation.[9] Later abolitionists, who called for immediate and unconditional emancipation, argued that gradualism was "wrong in theory, weak in practice, and fatally quieting to the conscience of the slaveholder."[10]

The conciliatory approach toward slave holders, the gradualist approach toward emancipation, and the theological counsel to blacks who were expected to live patiently with the system until the practice died out were based upon a desire to uphold a sense of harmony within the Quaker community in order to avoid unnecessary schism and social unrest. This conciliatory approach also appears to have been part of a tactic of social change that took into account that theologically the slaves and the slave holders were siblings in the sight of God. Although the attempt to foster a fraternal atmosphere in resolving the conflict over slavery has value, there is a lack of sensitivity to the plight of the enslaved that undermines the theological impact of the Quaker analysis of slavery as a sinful institution. To counsel patience to those who suffer while remaining untouched by that suffering raises questions about the counselors' faithfulness to the love-of-neighborhood ethic in the context of slavery.

EMANCIPATION *VS.* RACIAL UPLIFT

Dwight Dumond has noted some of the differences that separated black abolitionist from white abolitionists. One difference related was whether emancipation and racial uplift should be addressed together or were separate issues, with the latter coming much later. Dumond indicates that white abolitionists claimed that the only way to abolish slavery was to do it before proceeding to the task of elevating the race. Any consideration of particular plans following emancipation would allow the discussion to be drawn away from the main question, emancipation, thereby introducing "all sorts of extraneous issues."[11] Abolitionists in support of separating emancipation from racial uplift maintained that only as free men and women who enjoyed a full measure of civil rights could blacks cultivate their minds, accumulate property, discipline their habits, and assume responsibilities essential to correct social attitudes.[12] There is a certain logic to such a position, but given the context in which this argument was waged, namely, pervasive racism, questions regarding the inferiority of blacks, and concerns about whites and blacks living together on an equal basis, it seems that Dumond's assertion that "the great obstacle to the emancipation and elevation of the Negro was the prevailing belief in racial inferiority and biological inequality" says more about the validity of the abolitionists' proposed two-step process than logic might suggest at first sight.[13]

DIFFERING VIEWS OF SLAVERY AND FREEDOM

Jane and William Pease, historians of black history, cite differences in perceptions about the nature of freedom as a contributing factor in the tension between white and black abolitionists. They observe that several decades before the Civil War, some viewed the antislavery movement as monolithic. However, particularly after 1840, the abolitionist movement seemed rife with internal heresy and treason. Although the controversies tended to be personal or defined by issues that had already divided the predominately white antislavery crusade, the chasm that separated black abolitionist from white ones was greater.[14]

One difference between the two groups stemmed from the different way each group understood the meaning of freedom and slavery. Whites, especially those who had been reared in the moral environment of New England, understood slavery and freedom as polar absolutes.[15] Their heritage and present reality were shaped by the notion of individual liberty, as enshrined in the Declaration of Independence and fought for in the American Revolution.[16] At the other end of the spectrum stood slavery, which was viewed as an absolute evil, the total negation of freedom, the denial of tradition, and the antithesis of progress and American ideals.[17] The Peases argue that blacks defined freedom and slavery with greater complexity. From their existential experience and from history, blacks understood that slavery and freedom were not mutually exclusive, as separate from each other as righteousness from sin.[18]

As Jane and William Pease explain, certainly blacks did experience two extremes. At one pole they experienced absolutely no freedom as slaves. They could not decide how or where they would live, work, rear their families, order their personal relationships, or worship their God. At the opposite pole was freedom. In theory, free blacks had as many options as fully enfranchised, propertied, middle-class, white Americans. But, as the Peases contend, and as other scholars confirm, those descriptions of slavery and freedom are only the extremes. There was actually a range of experiences that made up the black experience at this time. Some slaves had a measure of freedom because they could hire out their own time and labor, with the permission of their masters. Some who were free were excluded from school apprenticeships; denied the vote; deemed ineligible to serve on a jury. Thus they were partially enslaved.[19]

One important issue that separated black abolitionists from their white counterparts was a huge difference in perceptions. Whites, because they conceived of their own freedom in absolutes, embraced a simple duality. The experience of blacks was neither simply slavery nor absolute freedom but "more or less freedom and more or less slavery."[20] The Peases note that although both groups pursued common goals of emancipation and civil equality, their different perceptions of slavery and freedom led to different perceptions of the relationship between those goals. Whites were committed to ending slavery, immediately and without compensation, for slavery was the root sin that stained the fabric of American society. To be sure, some whites felt that they must work to eliminate discrimination and prejudice as well.

However, even as some white abolitionists undertook this dual commitment, they often had the same racial attitudes as those who were not committed to them. Northern whites, who often treated free blacks in racist ways, were willing to accept political and social restrictions on the newly freed blacks when emancipation came. These whites were unaware of how much improvement was necessary within their own society. In such a context, antislavery activity did not ensure that blacks were viewed as brothers.[21]

The Peases and other scholars observe that Northern blacks, who were surrounded by prejudice, deprived of civil liberties, and barred from economic opportunity, rejected the notion that they were truly free. If poverty was an "immediate and visible sign" of the persistent effects of slavery, then white abolitionists were often oblivious of the fact that part of the struggle of emancipation involved fighting for economic justice in behalf of blacks. Blacks were steered to the most menial, least attractive, and minimally rewarding jobs. They were denied access to education, vocational training, and capital, which would have extended their options and enabled them to achieve economic parity with whites. White abolitionists tended to ignore this important dimension, while most blacks recognized the importance of economic justice.[22]

THE MORAL SUASION APPROACH

As the nation grew closer to the start of the Civil War, black and white abolitionists differed over the most effective means of ending slavery. From 1830 to the Civil War, whites attempted to change public opinion by moral suasion as a means of ending slavery in the South. White abolitionists like the Garrisonians focused on purging individual consciences of the sin and guilt of slavery. Jane and William Pease contend that this emphasis on the religious aspect of slavery by those complicit in the institution of slavery shaped their efforts into an ideological, abstract pattern that tended to forget blacks as individuals.[23] Both in the battle against slavery and in efforts to overcome prejudice, white abolitionists seemed to put the condition of their own souls first. The

Peases contend that although followers of Garrison were only a small fraction of white abolitionists, "nearly all abolitionists were more concerned with the institution of slavery than with the rights and well-being of Southern slaves or Northern freemen."[24]

This charge against white abolitionists, with respect to the seemingly negative influence of the theological underpinning of their abolitionist methodology, seems somewhat harsh, though not completely without foundation. In church historian Douglas M. Strong's study of the religious and political alliance of ecclesiastical abolition, we are given a carefully nuanced portrait of the pervasive influence of religious faith upon members of the Liberty Party.[25] Strong also gives a carefully articulated explanation of the forces that provided the theological grounding for the Liberty Party in a way that highlights the uniqueness of the party as a political entity, while illustrating how the interests of that party were consistent with the religious and political culture of the American context in the 1840s. Strong makes the case for the significance of religion and, specifically, a particular theological perspective that grounded the antislavery church movement in the central and western sections of New York.

For these antislavery churches, chattel slavery was viewed as a paradigm for tyrannical institutions that existed throughout society. The fact that major denominations and political parties refused to condemn slave holders was a clear indication that such institutions imposed chains upon the human conscience. Inasmuch as God's government could not be established through the instruments of these faulty human institutions, the only option was to secede from these religious institutions. Those who chose to defect from the major denominations were committed to establishing new, purified organizations, specifically, the Liberty Party and antislavery congregations. The defectors were attempting to make the polities of both the church and the state holy. These ecclesiastical abolitionists wanted to restructure not only the culture of American religion, but also the culture of American politics.

The theological underpinning for this movement among evangelicals was the popular doctrine of entire sanctification. Out of this belief in a "second blessing" beyond the initial "new birth" conversion through entire sanctification, it was possible for each believer and by extrapolation all of society to obey the moral law of God completely. These abolitionists, who were fueled by the powerful religious experience of evangelical perfection, were convinced that a sanctified life and a sanctified society could be realized after Christians separated from impure institutions.

This ecclesiastical movement was not limited to white abolitionists. Henry Highland Garnet, Samuel Ringgold Ward, William Wells Brown, and Frederick Douglass held leadership positions in the Liberty Party, which encouraged blacks to assume positions of power. In contrast to the major political parties of the time, the Liberty Party included socially marginalized persons, including the rural working class and women. From Strong's account, the portrait of this ecclesiastical abolitionism was broadly based in terms of its focus and goals. The institution of slavery constituted a paradigm for the major ills that afflict society. The goal was not just emancipation but a more just society.

Yet, Jane and William Pease have charged that nearly all abolitionists were concerned with the institution of slavery rather than individual blacks and that abolitionists were more concerned with saving their own souls than with the welfare of blacks. The theological framework from which these ecclesiastical abolitionists operated lends some credibility to these charges. One does not always get the sense that the activities of white abolitionists touched blacks in concrete ways or that the sufferings of slaves and the deprivation of free blacks per se motivated white antislavery activity. Analysis of the systematic dehumanization or demoralization of a segment of God's people does not appear in the account of the ecclesiastical abolitionists' story, particularly as they articulate their struggle against slavery. In Strong's account of the Liberty Party's development and demise, racial prejudice is acknowledged; there is, however, no account of how the religious faith or rhetoric of the party members sought to challenge the ideology of white supremacy. For black abolitionists engaged in the struggle, who also envisioned a just society, acknowledgment of their personhood, and securing the means of living their lives in full dignity *in concrete ways* were uppermost in their thinking. This kind of fundamental difference contributed to the misunderstandings that the Peases cite and elicited the frustration that blacks in the movement expressed about the abolitionist struggle as a genuinely interracial one.

RESISTANCE TO ALL-BLACK ANTISLAVERY
INSTITUTIONS

More friction would occur between black and white abolitionists over the Negro convention movement. By the 1840s the Negro convention movement had already been underway. These
conventions had addressed the "black laws" of various Northern
states, the advancement of free blacks, and the abolition of slavery. In time the national conventions were replaced by and large
by state conventions. "While white abolitionists engaged in fac-
tional dispute over the relationship of their movement to organized religion and other reform goals, the Negro convention
movement launched its campaign for the franchise."[26] The Peases
contend that whites largely ignored the suffrage issue, though I
note black involvement in the Liberty Party during its existence.
However, the Peases are correct when they state that whites immediately denounced the Negro conventions as racist separatism
within the antislavery movement. In response to the criticism of
whites, blacks argued that suffrage was central to American political life. It was a necessity for those seeking equal civil rights.
Thus its pursuit was viewed as a vital part of the quest for freedom.[27]

Scholar Shirley Yee identifies the differences between blacks
and whites in terms of their perspective on what constituted the
essentials within the struggle for abolition. For black abolitionists,
the issues of slavery and racism struck closer to home existen-
tially than for whites. Most blacks involved in the movement had
been former slaves, had relatives and friends who were still in
bondage, and had encountered racism in their lives. A major part
of their agenda went beyond just the ending of slavery. They were
also concerned about social, political, and economic equality,
which was integral to their agenda. They recognized that they
had to fight on a number of fronts in order to challenge racial
discrimination in American society. In addition, as a way of helping the free black community, they promoted temperance, moral
reform, and education. Black abolitionists were engaged in a number of activities: cooperating with whites when possible, organizing all-black antislavery societies, writing, speaking, petitioning,

and participating in self-help projects in their own neighbor-hoods.[28]

Yee contends that one of the major differences between black and white abolitionists centered on racism within the abolitionist movement. Although black, white, and racially mixed societies appeared in the Northeast, and in Ohio and Michigan, racism pervaded the movement. It prevented full and equal cooperation between the two races, for not all white abolitionists advocated racial equality. Even those who did sometimes were guilty of pa-tronizing attitudes toward their black colleagues.[29] She maintains that racism proved to be a "formidable barrier" between blacks and whites. This was manifested in ways ranging from "a myopic vision of abolitionists goals to the outright exclusion of blacks from white organizations and discrimination even in racially in-tegrated societies." There were even "several integrated antisla-very societies that maintained separate seating for blacks and whites at public events and a few white societies fought to keep blacks out altogether." Eventually, the problem of racism within organized abolitionism became public, as black leaders challenged their secondary status in the larger white movement. Yee cites Frederick Douglass's break with William Lloyd Garrison as part of this challenge, for Douglass advocated separatism from white abolitionism. Those blacks who broke with the Garrisonians were "fed up" with the discriminatory treatment of blacks in the move-ment and the failure of moral suasion to end slavery.[30]

Like Yee, George M. Fredrickson identifies racial prejudice as a major factor that hampered the abolitionist movement. White abolitionism was spawned by the evangelicalism of the Second Great Awakening and its millenarian or perfectionist offshoots.[31] But, Fredrickson observes, their own relations with blacks some-times revealed that white abolitionists were not entirely free of the aversive prejudice that was widespread in the North. He con-tends that what differentiated the Northern abolitionists from the rest of the North was their adherence to nonracial principles in the realm of public political and social organization. The most effective sanction for their position was a literal interpretation of the Declaration of Independence. If "all men are created equal" and "endowed by their creator with certain inalienable rights," then it was sheer hypocrisy for Americans to hold blacks as slaves and deny them the essential rights of citizenship.[32] However, many abolitionists, perhaps a majority, were not in fact convinced that blacks as a race were intellectually equal to whites. But to them, this consideration was basically irrelevant. This was because, like Thomas Jefferson, they grounded their belief in equality on the doctrine of an innate moral sense shared by all human beings rather than on an identity of rational capabilities.[33] Though white abolitionists condoned such "natural" inequalities as based on achievement and cultivation, they stood firmly against artificial barriers to the advancement of any individual or group. Thus, Fredrickson asserts, abolitionists failed to arouse much sympathy for blacks as human beings. However, their secondary contention–that slavery degraded free white labor and retarded capitalistic economic development by giving slave holders an unfair advantage in the competition for land, labor, and capital–struck a more responsive cord.[34]

Fredrickson's work on white perceptions of blacks in the nineteenth century helps to explain the difficulty of addressing the basic human rights of blacks, even within the white branch of the abolitionist movement. His study on racial thought between 1817 and 1914 provides support for the notion that black abolitionists had concrete reasons for their perception that addressing the debilitating effect of racism was crucial to attaining their goals for progress in American society. The discussion in the 1830s over the black personality and the prospects of blacks for success in American society had been, by and large, a dialogue between environmentalist defenders of a single human nature and proponents of deep-seated racial differences.[35]

ROMANTIC RACISM

In the 1840s and 1850s discussions of race increasingly started from a common assumption that the races differed fundamentally.[36] The biological school saw blacks as pathetically inept creatures who were slaves to their emotions and incapable of progressive development and self-government because they lacked the white man's enterprise and intellect.[37] However, those who gave priority to emotion rather than to thought, sanctioned both by romanticism and evangelical religion, came up with a strikingly different concept of black differences. Whereas scientists and practical-minded people saw only weakness, the more idealistic saw redeeming virtues and even evidence of superiority in blacks. Fredrickson viewed this as romantic racism. A number of white abolitionists could be characterized as romantic racists. Romantic racism acknowledged differences between the races but denied a notion of racial hierarchy.[38]

Fredrickson maintains that although romantic racists acknowledged that blacks were different from whites, and probably always would be, they projected an image of blacks that could be construed by some as flattering or laudatory. They endorsed the "child" stereotype of the most sentimental school of proslavery paternalism and plantation romances. However, they rejected slavery itself because it took unfair advantage of the so-called innocence and good nature of blacks. Further development of this position would later deny unequivocally that these traits constitute inferiority. The logical extreme of this position was to argue that blacks were the superior race because their docility constituted the ultimate in Christian virtue.[39] Fredrickson cites clergyman and abolitionist William Ellery Channing as an example of the romantic racist. In Channing's 1835 essay "Slavery" he used the "child" stereotype. Charles Stuart, in an article for the *Quarterly Antislavery American* (1836), also described blacks in romantic-racist terms as "eminently gentle, submissive, affectionate and grateful."[40]

Others even associated these alleged black virtues with Christianity, viewing the black as the "natural" Christian.[41] In 1842, Lydia Maria Child, editor of the *National Antislavery Standard*, who linked emancipation with women's suffrage, concluded that "the races of mankind are different, spiritually as well as physically."[42] Though she acknowledged the differences, she denied that they had always existed. She maintained that they were "the effects of spiritual influences, long operating on character, and in their turn becoming causes." For her the proper response to racial differences was a brotherly pluralism.[43]

By the early 1840s the antislavery movement provided fertile soil for romantic racism. Fredrickson maintains that the growth of romantic racism in antislavery circles can be accounted for in several ways. First, it was a reflection of the general trend of thought away from racial environmentalism and toward an acceptance of inherent diversity. It was a way of adjusting to this compelling idea that was apparently compatible with Christian humanitarianism and opposition to slavery. Further, it added strength to the antislavery argument to contend that slavery constituted oppression of "one of the best races of the human family." Beyond this, however, Fredrickson observes that for romantic racists, the black was a symbol of something that seemed tragically lacking in white American civilization. He states, "The idealized Negro was a convenient symbol to point up the deficiencies, not so much perhaps of the white race itself, but the racial self-image whites seemed in danger of accepting."[44]

Fredrickson identifies the heart of a critique of romantic racism when he asserts that benevolent reformers tended to see the black person more as a symbol than as a person, more as a vehicle for romantic social criticism than as a human being with the normal range of virtues and vices. He states: "A critical observer might also wonder how deeply and unequivocally white humanitarians really identified themselves with the stereotype of the submissive black. Meekness might be a virtue, but was it in fact the only virtue or even the cardinal one for those who celebrated its presence in the Negro?"[45]

Fredrickson suggests that Harriet Beecher Stowe provided the most influential expression of the image of the black as a natural Christian in her novel *Uncle Tom's Cabin.* For example, Uncle Tom, although not a typical slave, embodied that perfect gentleness and ability to forgive that are supposedly latent in the black and that will come to flower under favorable circumstances. Blacks were "confessedly more simple, docile, child-like and affectionate, than other races."[46] Fredrickson indicates that the romantic and "feminine" conception of the black character, as popularized by Harriet Beecher Stowe, was one of the factors that contributed to a revived interest in black expatriation or colonization in the 1850s. Her image of Africa as the future home of a peculiarly Christian and "feminine" civilization implied that American blacks should return to the environment where their special potentialities could be the most fully realized.[47]

Fredrickson asserts that the romantic-racist view of blacks and their role in American society, which was popular by 1864, was benevolent in intent and, generally speaking, not linked to an unequivocal theory of white supremacy. However, as characteristically put forth by whites, it often revealed "a mixture of cant, condescension, and sentimentality, not unlike the popular nine-teenth-century view of womanly virtue, which it so closely re-sembled."[48] The philosophy of romantic racism could be chal-lenged on a number of grounds. Fredrickson holds that it was a racial philosophy that could easily be transmuted into an overt doctrine of black inferiority. He also maintains that it was distin-guished from harsher forms of racism only by a certain flavor of humanitarian paternalism. That would seem to be an understate-ment.

I maintain that a striking error of romantic racism as it applies to white abolitionists harkens back to the criticism made in the beginning of this chapter with reference to Charles Sumner. The representation of blacks in romantic racism denies them the full range of human strengths and weaknesses. It does not allow for the differentiation between individuals. It treats the black as an abstraction rather than as a concrete person of flesh and blood. Although it is intended to be benign and positive, it denies the full humanity of blacks, as does the racist characterization of blacks as beasts or subhuman. The danger of romantic racism is in the insidious way it masks the dehumanizing quality that undergirds notions of casting groups into ideal types. In the end, because of this dehumanization, it is as bad, if not worse than, outright racial hatred. It is insidious because it has the capacity to fool the ro-mantic practitioner and deceive members of the idealized group. It reflects an attempt of the oppressing group to obscure the fact that racism is a pervasive element in the society itself, existing even in the heart of the well-intentioned "do-gooder." As Frantz Fanon has argued, "Racism is never a super-added element . . . [for] the social constellation, the cultural whole, are deeply modi-fied by the existence of racism."[49] If this is true, then no one from the oppressing group can escape its clutches completely.

Fredrickson does indicate that some of the original leaders of the white abolitionist movement, such as William Lloyd Garri-son, Theodore Weld, and Wendell Phillips, never succumbed openly to the romantic theory of racial differences. These men continued during the 1850s and through the Civil War to speak and act on the assumption that all human beings had the same basic psychology, possessed identical moral capabilities, and were likely to react in similar ways to common conditions. However, they made few explicit efforts during this period to combat the growing belief in innate racial differences, other than to object to those extremist uses of the notion that justified slavery and discrimination on the theory that blacks were radically inferior. Although they regarded slavery and racial discrimination as morally objectionable, and viewed equality as a moral concept and not one to be decided or even influenced by scientific or romantic speculations on the differing characteristics of whites and blacks, they failed to convince others that a sense of racial difference should in no way determine the status of American blacks. Fredrickson maintains that "the inability of the abolitionists to ground their case for the black man on a forthright and intellectually convincing argument for the basic identity in the moral and intellectual aptitudes of all races weakened their 'struggle for equality' and helps explain the persistence of racist doctrines after emancipation."[50]

According to Fredrickson, mid-nineteenth-century romantic racists were of two minds on the question of the ultimate destiny of blacks in America. Those most radical in their abolitionism saw blacks as permanent Americans who would make a special and valuable contribution to national life and character. Those admirers of blacks' "natural" Christianity believed that their only fulfillment would take place in Africa, and so they supported colonization as both necessary and desirable. This latter strain of romantic-racist thinking gained momentum in the 1850s as part of the growing segment of Northern opinion that opposed slavery but resisted the radical abolitionist demand that the black population be accepted after emancipation as a permanent and participating element in American society.[51]

Fredrickson asserts that many of those who were opposed to slavery, and who fought for its end, were unable to visualize a permanent future for blacks in America. For some, the ideal America was all white; others were willing to see blacks diminish and even disappear once they had served their purpose in Reconstruction. Thus, they might help free black Americans from slavery, but they would not promise full equality. Once again, emancipation as restoration of black dignity was not a concept that was necessarily a tenet of white abolitionism. For whites, there was a clear distinction between emancipation and full equality. As Fredrickson notes, "They . . . did not really regard Negroes as potential brothers; they viewed them rather as temporary and inferior sojourners in a white America, to be granted 'rights,' perhaps, but not the deeper acceptance reserved for members of 'the most vigorous and prolific race.'"[52]

WE *ARE* HUMAN!

In response to George Fredrickson, who examined the question of racial thought from the perspective of whites in the nineteenth century, Mia Bay has examined the question of racial thought from the perspective of African Americans in the same century. She provides a portrait from the perspective of blacks, both free and enslaved, educated and uneducated, who wrote of their experience of whites. In regard to those blacks who participated in the abolitionist movement, their experiences bore out that even whites known as "friends of the Negro" slowly came to accept the prevailing social and scientific arguments for black inferiority. Blacks, however, challenged white racial ideology from its eighteenth-century origins onward. Men and women in the antislavery movement reaffirmed the traditional scriptural conception of all people as children of God. They also opposed environmental explanations of black color and physiognomy, which argued that Africans were both so degraded and so different from Europeans that they should be seen as a lower species of people, suited only for perpetual slavery.[53]

Even early in abolitionism, blacks felt compelled to challenge racist assumptions that viewed blacks as subhuman. For example, Absalom Jones and Richard Allen, both former slaves, challenged racist assessments of black capacities in a 1794 essay published in the back of their "Narrative of the Proceedings of the Black People, During the Late Awful Calamity in Philadelphia in the Year 1793, and a Refutation of Some Censures, Thrown upon Them in Some Late Publications." In that essay (whose authors were listed as "A.J." and "R.A.") Jones and Allen, who were leaders of Philadelphia's Free African Society, challenged racists:

Those who stigmatize us as men, whose baseness is incurable try the experiment of taking a few black children, and cultivate their minds with the same care, and let them have the same prospect in view, as you would wish for your own children, you would find upon the trial, they were not inferior in mental endowments.[54]

Here we find the familiar theme of black abolitionism: concern for the dignity and worth of blacks as human beings. Bay observes that even in the early period of abolitionism (prior to 1830) a number of black writers clearly felt the need not only to defend their race's innate abilities but also to affirm the place of blacks in the human family.[55] Bay quotes an ex-slave on this point:

> Can it be contended, that a difference of colour alone can constitute a difference in species?—if not, in what single circumstance are we different from mankind? What variety is there in our organization? What inferiority of art in the fashioning of our bodies? What imperfection in the faculties of our minds?—Has not a negro eyes? Has not a negro hands, organs, dimensions, senses, affections, passions?[56]

From the late eighteenth century onward, blacks protesting slavery and racial discrimination pointedly reaffirmed the legitimate place of their race in the human species and cited the physical and mental characteristics shared by both races as evidence.[57] Bay asserts that proslavery and anti-black arguments for black inferiority were rejected by white abolitionists, but the attitudes and actions of individual whites in the abolitionist movement often failed to live up to the movement's egalitarian ideology. Further, while white abolitionists were staunchly antislavery, they were less reliable as allies against racism. Thus, Bay reiterates the fact that emancipation and racial equality were not synonymous to white abolitionists.

Blacks were sometimes unwelcome in the new white abolitionist societies that began to proliferate after 1830. An example was the Ladies' New York Anti-Slavery Society, established in 1835. It was led by middle-class evangelicals who opposed social mixing of the races and effectively excluded black members. Even integrated abolitionist organizations did not always admit blacks on equal terms. Blacks were allowed only limited role in the decisions of authority within them. Moreover, as the abolitionist movement grew, it attracted white supporters whose antislavery politics did not always entail a strong commitment to black equality.[58]

Bay quotes Theodore S. Wright, who wrote in *The Colored American* for October 14, 1837: "Three years ago, when a man professed to be an Abolitionist we all knew where he was. He was an individual who recognized the identity of the human family. Now a man calls himself an abolitionist and we know not where to find him."[59] Here, Wright suggests the bewilderment that he must have experienced as he reflected upon the racist thinking of even "friends of the Negro." Some black abolitionists avoided situations in which they might encounter a snub or rebuff within white abolitionist circles.

Bay concludes that in the face of color phobia, which was, she contends, so ubiquitous that it even compromised white allies in the antislavery movement, black thinkers became ever more determined to uphold traditional wisdom about the unity of the races. Despite the presence of racism, black abolitionists did not abandon their connections with white abolitionists.

THE BLACK ABOLITIONIST AS A SYMBOL

The black abolitionist was a symbol of the struggle for white abolitionists.[60] Many blacks in the movement were themselves former slaves, and they were called upon to share their experiences under slavery. It was the presence of blacks in the Garrisonian years of the movement that marked the greatest difference with earlier abolitionist effort, and so they had an important place in white abolitionism. In the earlier phase blacks were regarded as a recipient of good works rather than as an "expounder" of the faith, but from the 1830s onward blacks were viewed as expounders.[61] Although blacks were forming all-black societies, there was no substantial withdrawal of blacks from integrated societies. Indeed, many blacks were opposed to all-black auxiliaries, maintaining that such societies perpetuated the very evils they sought to combat, namely, prejudice and discrimination.[62]

The formation of all-black societies was not a reflection of a "go it alone" philosophy, although there was some strain in working in interracial organizations. In truth, the founders of black societies did not view their efforts as self-contained or distinctive. They viewed their role as a "true auxiliary," namely, supportive, supplemental, and subsidiary. Benjamin Quarles argues that there was an interlocking relationship between blacks and whites in the movement, which was demonstrated by the support, financial and otherwise, that they gave each other in pursuit of a common goal. Black societies, churches, and Sunday Schools supported the abolitionist movement, supplemented by individual contributions. The financial contributions of blacks were not large, but they came at an early time in the crusade and had a morale-building effect upon white comrades.[63] However, the social mingling of blacks and whites in the abolitionist movement had special perils.[64]

As Quarles observes, after the split of the American Anti-Slavery Society which led to the creation of the American and Foreign Anti-Slavery Society in 1833, blacks became more outspoken toward white crusaders. Although blacks had acknowledged the considerable debt they owed to their white comrades, they had always been aware of the latter's shortcomings. Blacks did charge many white abolitionists with harboring racial prejudice. To some black abolitionists, white participation in the cause reflected abstract issues the Northern whites had against Southern whites, not recognizing that they had prejudice in their own hearts. There were occasions when white abolitionists attended concerts or recitals from which blacks were barred or segregated. Additionally, some abolitionists, particularly during the formative 1830s, held that blacks should not be admitted to antislavery meetings or hold membership in the societies.[65] Quarles charges that "in reformist circles, as elsewhere, there was a strong undercurrent of anti-Negro sentiment, mirrored in the common preference for light-skinned Negroes over those of richer pigmentation."[66]

Quarles indicates that even when blacks and whites worked side by side, they seldom sustained a peer relationship. Blacks found whites to be paternalistic, with a tendency to over-praise black achievement, as if they were surprised that blacks had any ability at all. Further, like earlier abolitionists, these whites offered advice freely to blacks, and blacks viewed this as patronizing. As vexing as these things could be, the main complaint blacks had against white abolitionists was their half-heartedness in carrying out the second of their twin goals within emancipation—the elevation of free blacks.[67] Whites were slow to offer economic assistance and job opportunities to blacks. Quarles indicates that "most white abolitionists simply did not think in terms of the workingman, white or colored. . . . They never seemed to fully sense that economic freedom was coequal with, if not basic to, all other freedoms."[68]

Quarles also notes that by 1840 blacks had come to view many white abolitionists as having a tendency toward abstraction. William and Jane Pease concur, indicating that white abolitionists tended to view the movement as ideological warfare, in which the outcome was secondary to the stimulus of the mental jousting:

> To free blacks, white antislavery became ever more remote and abstract while their needs were immediate, concrete, and personal—not to be satisfied with ideological resolutions. . . . Blacks, whose very existence was threatened, found abstraction irrelevant; whites, plagued by guilt and prejudice, failed to comprehend the practical issues.[69]

It seemed to some blacks that whites viewed the focus of blacks on their immediate, material needs as manifesting self-interest rather than dedication to antislavery principles.[70] For the white abolitionists, to strike a moral posture seemed more important than to strike at slavery.[71] This tendency to abstraction appears to have been irritating to blacks, who could ill-afford the luxury of abstraction because their concerns were personal and existential. These problems became more evident to blacks after 1840, and they began to rely more on their own resources in the struggle. The black convention movement would take on an even stronger abolitionist character with the 1840 split in the American Anti-Slavery Society.[72] It is significant that after the split blacks reconsidered whether to go it alone, but the majority of blacks preferred to work with whites on abolition.[73]

ABOLITIONISM AS A JOINT EFFORT

Even though blacks and whites had different approaches, they continued to participate in predominately white antislavery societies up to the Civil War.[74] However, their increasingly divergent views led to "constant misunderstanding." Jane and William Pease contend that "neither white nor black quite comprehended the dual nature of the crusade which jointly they sought to wage, for their failure to communicate obscured the difference which tore them asunder."[75] In defining black abolitionism in this context, the Peases assert that black abolitionism was

> neither confined by a unified theory of opposition to sla-
> very nor limited to engagement within the framework of
> antislavery organizations and activities. Compared to its
> white counterpart, it more emphatically embraced practi-
> cal efforts to provide economic opportunity and social mo-
> bility for northern blacks, to acquire the franchise and in-
> sure civil rights, to establish a sense of black identity and
> community.[76]

What can we conclude about the nature of abolitionism as an interracial movement? How prevalent was racism within the movement itself, and what impact did racial prejudice have upon the accomplishments of the movement as a whole? Should it be surprising that racism could be found within abolitionism itself?

Black abolitionists have sometimes spoken of the racism that existed within the very reform movements designed to secure black emancipation. However, in his study of abolitionism and the religious tensions of American democracy, Douglas Strong distinguishes those members of the Liberty Party from other reformers. He maintains that from the party's inception, it championed a number of legislative proposals calculated to extend equal rights to all persons living in the United States. These proposals always began with the repudiation of slavery. During the course of the 1840s, however, party supporters realized that in addition to condemning the sin of slave-holding, they needed to dedicate themselves to ending racism and securing the full rights of citizenship for blacks and others.[77] Strong states:

> Unlike many other reformers, the perfectionist Liberty ac-
> tivist correctly understood that one of the fundamental anti-
> slavery problems to be addressed was racial injustice as well
> as legal emancipation. They were fearful that once African

Americans were emancipated they would be forced into a new servitude because of lingering prejudice, the absence of economic opportunity, and the lack of real political power.[78]

Strong does not identify the "other reformers"; thus, it is not clear that his observation specifically contradicts others with regard to white abolitionism in general. Other scholars have noted that the specter of racism was present in the reform efforts of some white abolitionists. Gerald Sorin makes an observation similar to that of Douglas Strong, with respect to abolitionists:

The abolitionists were agitators who hoped to convince their fellow Americans that slavery was morally wrong. They often disagreed among themselves, over both means and ends, but they were all dedicated to emancipation and concerned about the tragic human consequences of slavery, especially the victimization of blacks. Many abolitionists were equally committed to the goal of changing white America's negative consciousness about blacks in the hope of ending racial discrimination.[79]

In this opening paragraph of Sorin's book *Abolitionism,* the author does not indicate whether he is speaking of all abolitionists; however, based on the structure of the book, it becomes clear that when he speaks about abolitionism, in general, he is speaking primarily about white abolitionists. He does have a separate chapter on black abolitionism, suggesting that black abolitionism was a separate aspect of the larger, white-dominated movement. This is not an unusual approach to abolitionism. If we understand that Sorin is speaking primarily of white abolitionists, then the implication we can draw from his opening paragraph is that white abolitionists were dedicated to winning emancipation of blacks from slavery *and* were "equally committed" to fighting against racial discrimination. Sorin forces us to raise questions about his assertions as he proceeds with his study.

When he talks about the radicalism that captured a number of white abolitionists, including William Lloyd Garrison, he notes that there were "vital limits to their radicalism."[80] Sorin holds that the abolitionist cause never completely lost its association with paternalism. At this point, he does not articulate how this paternalism was manifested. But later, he observes:

> The great limiting factor for abolitionist growth was racism—a racism that knew no sectional or ideological boundaries. A belief in the inferiority of the black pervaded the consciousness of white America; abolitionists themselves did not escape it entirely. This belief, whether or not it was culturally ingrained in whites prior to the enslavement of blacks, was certainly heightened by slavery, which degraded and brutalized its victims. Furthermore, as slavery became more entrenched and its social and economic advantages more apparent, white men found it harder to give up.[81]

Here Sorin concedes not only the presence of racism in American society but that white abolitionists did not escape its influence. In his chapter on black abolitionism, Sorin observes:

> White abolitionists sincerely desired and were working for true black equality after emancipation, and the Liberty party devoted much of its time to the "black problem" in the North. But many abolitionists never outgrew a paternalistic racism; their efforts for integration were most often abortive and were not generally undertaken in the important area of economic equality. . . . Blacks had sorrowfully learned that many white abolitionists . . . had a tendency to emphasize long-range, abstract goals. Blacks therefore came to see their task as ensuring that the abolitionists never forgot the immediate practical needs of the persecuted "free people of color." If the goal of abolitionism was to teach the white community that a society based on racial justice and brotherly love was feasible, white abolitionists would have to eliminate the cord of caste from their own bosoms and be consistent with their stated beliefs. White abolitionists would have to be pushed to "lay the ax right down at the root of the tree."[82]

Sorin's discussion of racism within the context of abolitionism suggests that, on the one hand, he gives considerable credit to white abolitionists in terms of their goals regarding emancipation, suggesting that they shared with blacks the goal of affirming black equality within American society. On the other hand, however, he is not only cognizant of the degree of racial prejudice in American society as a whole during the long period of abolitionism, but he is also aware of the presence of racism within the abolitionist movement itself. Sorin's acknowledgment of "paternal racism" within abolitionism helps to build the case that while white abolitionists fought in varying degrees for the abolition of slavery, the restoration of black dignity by the recognition of blacks' full humanity was not necessarily a concomitant aspect of their understanding of emancipation.

Herman E. Thomas, another scholar who addresses the prevalence of racism in the abolitionist movement, also notes that although blacks held views similar to their white counterparts on slavery and how it might be abolished, black abolitionists were confronted with race prejudice in the abolition movement itself.[83] He maintains that the Garrisonian and radical camps were accused of being insensitive to the question of race. Blacks were frequently excluded from the speaker's platform when it was known that they would talk about problems of race. Black abolitionist James McCune Smith believed that white abolitionists had forgotten for whom the fight against slavery was being waged. He once stated, "My dark face is one of the grievances on which all the pennies are collected. . . . No blacks, no coppers."[84] Earlier, he had stated that "until [white] abolitionists eradicate prejudice from their own hearts, they can never receive the unwavering confidence of the people of color."[85] In 1839 black abolitionist William Whipper was quoted as saying, "The national prejudice has so complexionally separated the interests of the people of this nation, that when those of opposite complexion meet with each other . . . it is next to impossible to divine their meaning and intent."[86] Herman Thomas contends that white abolitionists, whether they were Garrisonian, radical, anti-Garrisonian, or conservative, never received the full confidence of black people in the crusade against slavery. Even so, blacks like Remond, Smith, Whipper, and Garnet worked for the cause, at times side by side with Garrison and the Tappan brothers.

What conclusions can we draw? We can acknowledge that racial prejudice was indeed a problem, even within abolitionism. Blacks spoke of the pervasiveness of prejudice and denounced it. Clearly, it was far easier for them to perceive racism than it was for whites, for blacks were far more conscious of the assaults to their dignity, large and small, in a way that whites could not be. Whites may have abhorred slavery, but equality was not a necessary corollary. A reform movement often finds it difficult to see the splinter in its own eye, as it beholds the beam in its opponent's. The so-called pervasiveness of racism, even within reform movements, only suggests an even greater pervasiveness of racism within the larger society, especially if it is accurate that the percentage of abolitionists in the North was no more than 1 percent.[87] The whole culture was corrupted by racism. This flaw may well have weakened the moral power of the movement as a whole to tackle slavery.

The writings of black abolitionists indicate their perception of racism and their testimony to its destructive power upon them. The reflections of Douglass, the Fortens, Stewart, Lawrence, and our four featured freedom fighters make the point that restoration of black dignity as full human beings was of critical importance in their abolitionist struggle. To them, the enemy was racism, wherever they found it. Addressing the dehumanization in the lives of the enslaved and the quasi-free was their ultimate goal, beyond securing legal emancipation. Without attention to restoration of their status within the human family, emancipation would not mean much. The lives of most of the quasi-free had already attested to that reality.

Chapter 11

The Quest Unfulfilled

To be human, at the most profound level, is to encounter honestly the inescapable circumstances that constrain us, yet muster the courage to struggle compassionately for our own unique individualities and for more democratic and free societies. . . . What it means to be human is preeminently existential—a focus on particular, singular, flesh-and-blood persons grappling with dire issues of death, dread, despair, disease and disappointment.
—Cornel West, *The Cornel West Reader*

With respect to the place of African Americans in society, subsequent historical events in the United States have borne out that this quest for the restoration of their human dignity, inherent in the black abolitionist cause, was largely unfulfilled. The end of the Civil War left blacks emancipated but still less than second-class citizens. The Reconstruction period, which some thought would allow for the elevation of blacks, instead saw the emergence of Jim Crow, a legalized, segregated system in the South (with de facto segregation in the North), that would necessitate the modern civil rights movement. Although this movement brought civil and political relief to the African American community, it failed to address the legacy and current impact of white supremacy (racism) in American society. This demonstrates that although social, political, economic, and legislative measures may ameliorate the worst effects of racism, white supremacy is a demon that may be driven out—in the end—only "by prayer and

148

fasting."[1] Even so, persistence in the struggle against all odds, the legacy that black abolitionists have left to us, requires that we keep hope alive.

It was not enough to have opposed slavery, although certainly credit is due to those who did oppose slavery, given the evident difficulty there was in ending that institution. But did white abolitionists meet the criteria for a truly humanitarian stance in their opposition to black slavery? Their failure to recognize, unconditionally and without reservations, the full humanity of blacks and to affirm that humanity in the face of social, political, and economic pressures to do otherwise had serious consequences. It contributed to the failure of Reconstruction and accounts for the fact that the plight of blacks remained dismal and substandard through the remainder of the nineteenth century and well into the twentieth century. It made the modern civil rights movement a moral necessity.

If it was not enough to oppose slavery in the past without continuing the fight against racial injustice into the full range of American institutions, including the Christian church, then it is not enough now to maintain that slavery is "all in the past" and that the modern civil rights movement somehow has rendered the complaints of African Americans null and void. The specter of racism continues to loom large in the consciousness of the black community. The ideology of race is still operative; it still threatens black people because whites fail to accord them equality of respect and to grant them a *full* opportunity to participate in American society. This perception on the part of those of African descent—that they are still not viewed as equal participants in the American experiment because of their race—continues into the twenty-first century. For a good number of African Americans, W. E. B. Du Bois's assertion that "the problem of the color line" was *the* problem of the twentieth century remains relevant for *this* century. Furthermore, the notion that blacks experience the "peculiar sensation" of a "double consciousness" is still an existential reality as well.[2] This nagging sense of unfinished business, this painful feeling of a wound that refuses to heal, has been an issue that has occupied contemporary black religious thinkers over the last forty years.

BLACK THEOLOGIANS ECHO
THE CALL FOR BLACK DIGNITY

Black ethicist George D. Kelsey, writing from within a Christian context, analyzed racism in blunt theological terms that reiterated the absurd, mind-numbing, devastating contradiction that blacks pondered under the oppressive system of American slavery in the nineteenth century–at a time when proponents of slavery viewed America as a Christian nation. In the early 1960s Kelsey argued that race is not simply a social problem but a form of idolatrous "faith, that elevates race–a human factor–to the level of the ultimate. Racism is a god that has become the ultimate center of value for those who subscribe to it."[3] It alone is among the idolatries that call into question the creative action of God. In his masterful theological critique of racism, Kelsey sought to demolish the idol of white supremacy and to restore the notion of black dignity as something only God can confer; something that no human can rightfully deny.

Kelsey has not been alone in this preoccupation with the nature of black humanity as a key theme in black theological reflection. More recently, in a systematic theology text designed for African Americans, James H. Evans devotes a chapter to the theme of what it means to be human in black theology. Cognizant of black history in America, he too seeks to affirm that a critical issue for blacks in relation to their life of faith and action is the notion of black dignity. Evans affirms Kelsey's notion of racism as a form of idolatry that errs toward naturalism and contends that "to define a person on the basis of his or her physical distinctions tends toward biological determinism, undergirded by individual assumptions, and leads to the conclusion that whatever a person is or is to become is completely programmed in her or his genetic makeup."[4]

In contrast to this naturalism, Evans maintains that in the black experience the quest for identity leads to a consideration of one's relation to God; we discover who we are only in relation to God the Creator, in whose image all humans are made.[5] Moreover, the common foundation and goal of human existence are exemplified in the life and ministry of Jesus Christ, God who became human. This affirmation that Evans makes is what nineteenth-century freedom fighters such as Walker, Pennington, Garnet, and Ward clearly understood even in the face of oppression.

James H. Cone, like James Evans, has written a systematic theology text for African Americans. Cone devotes a chapter to defining the human being in the context of black theology. For black theology the black condition is the fundamental datum of human experience; the concreteness of human oppression in the world in which blacks are condemned to live is a context that cannot be treated lightly.[6] More than one hundred and twenty years after the emancipation of black slaves (Cone was writing in 1986), their descendants are still wrestling against the demon of racial prejudice in America. Cone understands racism as "a heresy," "a disease that perverts one's moral sensitivity and distorts the intellect."[7] He examines what it means to be human in black theology and concludes that it is in the context of oppression that blacks come to know what it means to be human:

> Only the oppressed know what human personhood is because they have encountered both the depravity of human behavior from oppressors and the healing powers revealed in the Oppressed One (Jesus Christ). Having experienced the brutality of human pride, they will speak less of human goodness; but also having encountered the meaning of liberation, they can and must speak of human worth as revealed in the black community itself affirming its blackness.[8]

For Cone, what it means to be human cannot be addressed in the abstract but has to be understood within a particular context to ensure that one speaks of individual, real persons, rather than the universal human being, which does not exist. Cone contends that oppression is the key for understanding what it means to be human, for understanding what it is that makes human beings what they are, because the one human being who truly embodies what it means to be human is Jesus Christ, the God who became an oppressed Jew, thereby disclosing that both human nature and divine nature are inseparable from oppression and liberation.[9] As Cone reflects on the nature of human personhood, the memory of black enslavement and the persistence of racial oppression permeate his understanding of how one can speak about black humanness in spite of the oppressive elements that seek to devalue or even annihilate that existence.

Cone, as well as Evans, Kelsey, and other black theologians, is gripped with the same existential distress that gripped black abolitionists a century earlier. Although the conflict brings existential angst and a testing of faith, Cone finds, as Walker, Pennington, Garnet, and Ward did, that "God in Jesus meets us in the situation of our oppressed condition and tells us not only who God is and what God is doing about our liberation, but also who we are and what we must do about white racism."[10]

This conviction, fueled by faith, assures Cone, as it assured the four freedom fighters we have discussed, that the struggle against oppression, racism, and other societal enslavement is a righteous fight, that "their liberation is the manifestation of God's activity." Freedom, for Cone, is tied to liberation: "To be human is to be free, and to be free is to be human."[11] The truly free are those who fight against everything that opposes integral humanity; thus, paradoxically, "only the oppressed are truly free." To engage in the struggle for the liberation of the oppressed is to begin the process of restoration of what has been degraded because of one's identification with Jesus, the Oppressed One, who lives to deliver the oppressed.[12]

A QUEST UNFULFILLED

The works of Kelsey, Evans, Cone, and other religious thinkers of African descent bear witness that the struggle against black dehumanization continues. They offer a prophetic word to a church and to a culture that are still ensnared in the thick web of white supremacy. Allegiance to this idol still operates within American social structures to perform its death-dealing work on the humanity not only of blacks but of other people of color. Nearly one hundred years ago W. E. B. Du Bois spoke of "the shadow of a deep disappointment which rests upon the Negro people." Sadly, despite "whatever good has come in the years of change," that disappointment still remains.[13] The failure to affirm blacks' full humanity, even in contemporary times, and to own up to the specter of a more subtle but no less insidious brand of white supremacy in the present accounts for the persistent undercurrent of unrest that remains in the black psyche in the post–civil rights movement era. It is behind the anger in a good deal of the black community over attempts to dismantle affirmative action, distrust of the judicial system, the frustration over the phenomenon of "driving while black," the periodic brouhahas over the flying of the Confederate flag in the South, and the growing drumbeat for reparations.

The failure to acknowledge the full humanity of blacks has fostered an undercurrent of dissatisfaction that manifests itself not only in the perpetually disaffected underclass of blacks but even in the corporate halls and the academy. This dissatisfaction can make a middle-class black lawyer write: "Regardless of how much money I make as a corporate attorney, the impact of slavery is still here. We don't have the dignity and the respect we deserve as humans."[14] Full civil and political rights and economic opportunities are crucial for the advancement of African Americans. However, these material assets do not, in the final analysis, heal the wound that remains such a painful part of the story of the black presence in America. It is not until their full humanity is recognized and honored in all dimensions of life in America that its citizens can say that this country's legacy of black slavery and Jim Crow are truly things of the past. As Conrad Worrill, chairman of the National Black United Front in Calumet Park, Illinois, said in 2002: "The fact that this country, founded on the ideals of freedom, could spend centuries importing and breeding human beings as chattel, set them 'free' and then say, 'forget about it,' is not only unforgettable, it's unforgivable."[15]

What do blacks *really* want? They want to be treated as full human beings and to be accorded the same rights and privileges that are bestowed upon white people without question or hesitation. They want "the freedom of life and limb, the freedom to work and think, the freedom to love and aspire," without that freedom being viewed as "a problem."[16] They want that freedom of human life understood as something to which they are rightly entitled because they are indeed human. They want the recognition, in word and deed, that they too have been created in the image of God. They want acknowledgment that in rhetoric and praxis the *imago Dei,* a universal gift from God, cannot be morally denied to anyone on any basis, including race. They want recognition that the violation of this dignity, whether blatantly or subtly, distorts the human spirit and deforms the personality of all, not only the violated but the violators as well. They want it understood that the inner life of African Americans is as deep and profound as that of any other group of people. The denial of opportunities and the rejection of personhood, with significant numbers of the black community being consigned to inferior neighborhoods, educational facilities, and social services, create as great a degree of suffering in the souls of black folks as they would in the souls of whites. In short, black people want, as moral philosopher Raimond Gaita writes, the full dimension of social justice that cries from the heart: "Treat us as a human being, fully as your equal, without condescension."[17] Only when America as a whole repents of all that impedes the black quest for full justice can the rift between the races finally heal.

The quotation from Cornel West that serves as the epigraph for the present chapter epitomizes in a poignant yet empowering way the nature of what the black abolitionist struggle was about at its core. David Walker, James W. C. Pennington, Henry Highland Garnet, and Samuel Ringgold Ward represent not only the abolitionists who have made it into some black history texts but also the countless men, women, and children who participated in America's *first* civil rights movement: black abolitionism. Although West's definition of what it means to be human evokes the struggles of the past, it was intended to speak broadly to the nature of human struggle in contemporary times as well. The struggle to live authentic lives is certainly not limited to African Americans, for peoples of every nation, in the past and in the present, have been called upon to embrace that struggle. However, only those who dedicate themselves in some way or another to safeguard the dignity of the others, as well as themselves, truly exemplify what it means to be fully human. Until the affirmation of blacks as fully human becomes something that truly "goes without saying," the quest for acknowledgment of black dignity that occupied nineteenth-century black abolitionists remains unfulfilled.

Notes

Introduction

1. See Robert P. Kraynak, "Made in the Image of God: The Christian View of Human Dignity and Political Order," in *In Defense of Human Dignity: Essays for Our Times*, ed. Robert P. Kraynak and Glenn Tinder (Notre Dame, IN: University of Notre Dame Press, 2003), 81–118; Timothy P. Jackson, "A House Divided, Again: Sanctity vs. Dignity in the Induced Death Debates," in Kraynak and Tinder, *In Defense of Human Dignity*, 139–63; Francis Fukuyama, *Our Posthuman Future: Consequences of the Biotechnology Revolution* (New York: Farrar, Straus and Giroux, 2003); and Raimond Gaita, *A Common Humanity: Thinking about Love and Truth and Justice* (London: Routledge, 2000).

2. See Millard J. Erickson, *Christian Theology* (Grand Rapids, MI: Baker Book House, 1985), 495–517. In his discussion of theological anthropology Erickson identifies three classifications of views with respect to the nature of the image of God in human beings. The substantive view identifies the image with a trait or particular characteristics that humans possess, such as the capacity to reason. The relational view denies that the image of God is a characteristic or set of traits; it maintains that human beings' capacity to be in relation to God and to other human beings constitutes the *imago Dei*. The functional view holds that neither trait nor capacity for relationship constitutes the *imago Dei*, but rather the image of God is reflected in what human beings can do, such as exercise dominion over the rest of the created order.

3. David Walsh uses the phrases "ultimate worth" and "infinite value," which are quite common in contemporary theological reflection ("Are Freedom and Dignity Enough? A Reflection on Liberal Abbreviations," in Kraynak and Tinder, *In Defense of Human Dignity*, 171). Although I want to affirm that the value of a human being is high and inestimable or incalculable, I also recognize human beings as creatures who are fallen. "Ultimate worth" and "infinite value" are descriptors more appropriately ascribed to divinity than to humanity.

4. See Raimond Gaita, *A Common Humanity*, 67, 78. Gaita concedes that this capacity can be diminished by mental impairment or can be undetected in the case of severe mental retardation. However, as an

unimpaired human being the person would have the capacity for such an inner life. See his discussion of an incident in a psychiatric hospital in the early 1960s (17–20).

5. Gaita, *A Common Humanity*, xx.

6. Ibid.

7. Ibid., 82, emphasis added.

8. Ibid., 72.

9. Ibid.

10. Blacks knew within themselves that they were fully human, and black Christians believed that their dignity as human beings was a gift granted to them by God.

11. Benjamin Quarles, *Black Abolitionists* (1969; reprint, Cambridge, MA: Da Capo Press, 1991), 13.

12. Dwight Lowell Dumond, *Antislavery Origins of the Civil War in the United States* (Ann Arbor, MI: University of Michigan Press, 1959), 24.

13. Ibid., 24.

1. North American Slavery

1. Dwight Lowell Dumond, *Antislavery Origins of the Civil War in the United States* (Ann Arbor, MI: University of Michigan Press, 1959), 3.

2. David Brion Davis, *The Problem of Slavery in Western Culture* (New York: Oxford University Press, 1984), 33.

3. Ibid., 47.

4. Ibid., 46.

5. Milton C. Meltzer, *Slavery: A World History* (New York: Da Capo, 1993), 45.

6. Leon F. Litwack, *North of Slavery: The Negro in the Free States, 1790–1860* (Chicago: The University of Chicago Press, 1961), 3.

7. Arthur Zilversmit, *The First Emancipation: The Abolition of Slavery in the North* (Chicago: The University of Chicago Press, 1967), 7.

8. Ibid.

9. Ibid., 4.

10. Ibid., 6.

11. Dwight N. Hopkins, *Down, Up, and Over: Slave Religion and Black Theology* (Minneapolis: Fortress Press, 2000), 22.

12. Ibid., 23.

13. Zilversmit, *The First Emancipation*, 4.

14. Louis Filler, *Slavery in the United States* (New Brunswick: Transaction Publishers, 1998), 15.

15. Ibid., 15, 16.

16. Davis, *The Problem of Slavery in Western Culture*, 10.

17. Ibid.

18. Ibid., 30.

19. David Brion Davis, *The Problem of Slavery in the Age of Revolution (1770–1823)* (Ithaca, NY: Cornell University Press, 1975), 40. The contradictions lay in terms of whether the slaves were persons or property or some curious combination of both.

20. Ibid., 41.

21. Davis, *The Problem of Slavery in Western Culture*, 60.

22. Ibid., 31.

23. Ibid., 60.

24. Ibid., 255.

25. Don E. Fehrenbacher, *The Dred Scott Case: Its Significance in American Law and Politics* (1978; Oxford: Oxford University Press, 2001), 11.

26. Ibid., 12.

27. Ibid., 11–12.

28. Ibid., 12.

29. Ibid.

30. Ibid.

31. Ibid., 12–13.

32. Ibid., 13.

33. Ibid.

34. Fehrenbacher, *The Dred Scott Case*, 13. Arthur Zilversmit concurs with the notion that slavery existed in New England although there was no strong need for slave labor. Zilversmit names several factors that contributed to keeping the slave population small in New England: New England's lack of currency; its predominant pattern of small-scale agriculture; and the region's hostility to all foreigners, black and white. Also, it was more profitable for New Englanders to sell their cargo in the plantation colonies than to engage in the slave trade (see Zilversmit, *The First Emancipation*, 3).

35. Fehrenbacher, *The Dred Scott Case*, 13.

36. Ibid., 14.

37. Ibid., 15.

38. Ibid.

39. Ibid.

40. Ibid.

41. Ibid.

42. Ibid., 16.

43. Ibid.

44. Stanley M. Elkins, *Slavery: A Problem in American Institutional and Intellectual Life*, 2nd ed. (Chicago: The University of Chicago Press, 1968), 36.

45. Ibid.

46. Ibid.

47. Ibid., 37.

48. Ibid.

49. Ibid.

50. Elkins, *Slavery*, 38. Elkins bases his discussion on an essay by Oscar and Mary Hendlin, "Origins of the Southern Slave System."

51. Ibid., 81.

52. Ibid.

53. Dumond, *Antislavery Origins of the Civil War in the United States*, 44.

54. Ibid., 52.

55. Gerald Sorin, *Abolitionism: A New Perspective* (New York: Praeger Publishers, 1972), 19.

56. Ibid., 23.

57. Ibid., 37.

58. John Hope Franklin, *From Slavery to Freedom: A History of Negro Americans*, 5th ed. (New York: Alfred A. Knopf, 1980), 122.

59. Ibid., 134.

60. Ibid., 149.

61. Ibid., 150.

2. Seasons of Abolitionism

1. Gerald Sorin, *Abolitionism: A New Perspective* (New York: Praeger Publishers, 1972), 17.

2. Ibid., 18. Sorin also notes that for some abolitionists this impulse was developed out of less than noble motives, such as restrictive, paternalistic concerns and fear.

3. Dwight Lowell Dumond, *Antislavery Origins of the Civil War in the United States* (Ann Arbor, MI: University of Michigan Press, 1959), 24–25.

4. Dumond's discussion on this point suggests a cleaner break with slavery in the North than might be warranted. Resistance to abolitionism in the North remained an issue for some time afterward.

5. Dumond, *Antislavery Origins of the Civil War in the United States*, 5.

6. Ibid.

7. Ibid., 6. Historians differ on this. While Massachusetts, Connecticut, Pennsylvania, New Jersey, Rhode Island, and New Hampshire abolished slavery before 1800, New York did not do so until 1827 (see Johnnie Miles et al., eds., *Educator's Sourcebook of African American Heritage* [Paramus, NJ: Prentice Hall, 2001]). John Hope Franklin notes that the law prohibiting the African slave trade was passed on March 2, 1807. However, the traffic in African slaves was merely driven underground (see John Hope Franklin, *From Slavery to Freedom: A History of Negro Americans*, 5th ed. [New York: Alfred A. Knopf, 1980], 104).

8. Dumond, *Antislavery Origins of the Civil War in the United States*, 6. Dumond indicates that Virginia had raised the issue of discontinuing slavery but faltered. It was the only southern state to raise it.

9. Franklin, *From Slavery to Freedom,* 186.

10. Thomas E. Drake, *Quakers and Slavery in America* (New Haven, CT: Yale University Press, 1950), 4. Drake observes that the Mennonites, Moravians, and other small European groups akin to the Quakers also refrained from slave-holding in America from the beginning, but they came later than the Quakers and had no appreciable influence on public policy.

11. Ibid., 78.

12. Ibid., 100.

13. Ibid., 112.

14. Julie Winch, *A Gentleman of Color: The Life of James Forten* (Oxford: Oxford University Press, 2002), 188.

15. Franklin, *From Slavery to Freedom,* 176.

16. Winch, *A Gentleman of Color,* 188.

17. Franklin, *From Slavery to Freedom,* 117.

18. Ibid., 179.

19. Ibid., 178.

20. Martin R. Delaney, cited in Franklin, *From Slavery to Freedom,* 179.

21. Benjamin Quarles, *Black Abolitionists* (1969; reprint, Cambridge, MA: Da Capo Press, 1991), 14.

22. Ibid., 23, 24. The three blacks who participated were James McCrummell, Robert Purvis, and James Barbados.

23. Ibid., 198. The other measures were (1) California should enter the Union as a free state; (2) the other territories would be organized without mention of slavery; (3) Texas would cede certain lands to New Mexico and be compensated; and (4) there would be no slave trade in the District of Columbia (see Franklin, *From Slavery to Freedom,* 200).

24. The Fugitive Slave Law of 1793 allowed a slave holder to present the alleged fugitive slave before a judge without the benefit of a warrant. The slave was permitted neither a trial by jury nor given an opportunity to present witnesses to give testimony on his or her behalf. At the word of the slave holder, the judge could issue a certificate of repossession to the master (see Quarles, *Black Abolitionists,* 144).

25. Paul Johnson, *A History of the American People* (New York: HarperCollins Publishers, 1997), 400.

26. Quarles, *Black Abolitionists,* 199.

27. Ibid., 205.

28. Ibid.

29. George M. Fredrickson, *The Black Image in the White Mind: The Debate on Afro-American Character and Destiny, 1817–1914* (Hanover, NH: Wesleyan University Press, 1971), 117.

30. Franklin, *From Slavery to Freedom,* 201.

31. Ibid.

32. Frederick Douglass, cited in Quarles, *Black Abolitionists,* 231.

33. Ibid., 239.

34. See Quarles, *Black Abolitionists,* 235, 237.

35. Ibid., 240–41. Pennington's editorial was published in *The Weekly Anglo-American,* November 5, 1859.

36. See Johnson, *A History of the American People,* 460.

37. Sorin, *Abolitionism,* 147.

38. Ibid., 148.

39. Ibid., 102.

40. Ibid., 152, 153.

41. Ibid., 153.

42. Ibid., 155.

43. See Sorin, *Abolitionism,* 156.

44. See C. Vann Woodward, *The Strange Career of Jim Crow,* commemorative ed. (Oxford: Oxford University Press, 2002), 6.

3. Abolitionism in Black and White

1. See Gerald Sorin, *Abolitionism: A New Perspective* (New York: Praeger Publishers, 1972), 19.

2. Herman E. Thomas, *James W. C. Pennington: African American Churchman and Abolitionist* (New York: Garland Publishing, 1995), 103. The classification system is taken from Aileen S. Kraditor, *Means and Ends in American Abolitionism: Garrison and His Critics on Strategy and Tactics, 1834–1850* (New York: Pantheon Books, 1969), chap. 1. It is important to note that Kraditor's study does not cover abolitionism beyond 1850 (cf. Thomas, *James W. C. Pennington,* 105).

3. Thomas, *James W. C. Pennington,* 104. Quotation from Kraditor, *Means and Ends in American Abolitionism,* 8.

4. Thomas, *James W. C. Pennington,* 104.

5. Ibid.

6. Ibid., 105. Herman Thomas contradicts this assessment on page 105 when he writes, "William L. Garrison was probably the best representative of a 'Garrisonian' abolitionist." Yet in the next sentence he again describes Garrison in the same terms as a "radical." Thomas's instincts are correct with regard to his earlier description of Garrison's beliefs as being in line with the "radical" category. See also Henry Mayer, *All on Fire: William Lloyd Garrison and the Abolition of Slavery* (New York: St. Martin's Griffin, 2000).

7. Ibid.

8. Ibid., 105.

9. Ibid., 106.

10. Ibid.

11. Ibid.

12. Ibid., 106–7.

13. Ibid., 107.

14. Ibid.

15. Ibid., 108. Thomas indicates that one researcher has determined that records do not show that Remond ever withheld his taxes.

16. Ibid., 108.

17. Ibid., 108-9.

18. Ibid., 109.

19. Note that political abolitionist is not one of Kraditor's categories.

20. Thomas, *James W. C. Pennington,* 109. As quoted in Carleton Mabee, *Black Freedom: The Nonviolent Abolitionist from 1830 through the Civil War* (New York: Macmillan, 1970), 36-38.

21. Thomas, *James W. C. Pennington,* 109.

22. Whipper, as quoted in Mabee, *Black Freedom,* 36, 38; in Thomas, *James W. C. Pennington,* 109.

23. Thomas, *James W. C. Pennington,* 109.

24. Ibid., 109-10.

25. Ibid.

26. Ibid. Taken from Earl Ofari, *"Let Your Motto Be Resistance": The Life and Thought of Henry Highland Garnet* (Boston: Beacon Press, 1972), 30.

27. Thomas, *James W. C. Pennington,* 110.

28. Ibid., 105.

29. Ibid.

30. Ibid., 112.

31. Ibid., 113.

32. Ibid., 113-14.

33. Stanley M. Elkins, *Slavery: A Problem in American Institutional and Intellectual Life,* 2nd ed. (Chicago: The University of Chicago Press, 1968), 178.

34. Ibid.

35. Elkins, *Slavery,* 179.

36. Ibid., 179-80.

37. Ibid., 180.

4. David Walker

1. James Turner, "Introduction," in David Walker, *Appeal to the Coloured Citizens of the World, But in Particular, and Very Expressly, to Those of the United States of America* (Baltimore, MD: Black Classic Press, 1993), 12.

2. Ibid., 13. See also Julie Winch, *A Gentleman of Color: The Life of James Forten* (Oxford: "Oxford University Press, 2002), 245.

3. Turner, "Introduction," 13.

4. Benjamin Quarles, *Black Abolitionists* (1969; reprint, Cambridge, MA: Da Capo Press, 1991), 16.

5. Turner, "Introduction," 13.

6. Ibid., 12-13.

7. Ibid., 17.
8. Walker, *Appeal*, 20, 21, 27, 29, 37, 60, 92, 94.
9. Ibid., 20.
10. Ibid., 22.
11. Ibid., 49, 61, 63, 65, 91. Walker mentions the word *avarice* a number of times in the text.
12. Ibid., 70.
13. Ibid., 30.
14. Ibid., 45.
15. Ibid., 46.
16. Ibid., 57–63, 75.
17. Ibid., 56.
18. Ibid.
19. Ibid., 94, 95.
20. Ibid., 26, 36–37, 48, 85.
21. Ibid., 26.
22. Ibid., 36.
23. Ibid., 27, 88.
24. Ibid., 32.
25. Ibid., 33, 39, 74.
26. Ibid., 68.
27. Ibid., 80–81.
28. Ibid., 81.
29. Ibid., 40.
30. Ibid., 50.
31. Ibid., 35.
32. Ibid., 37–38.

5. James W. C. Pennington

1. See James W. C. Pennington, "The Fugitive Blacksmith; or, Events in the History of James W. C. Pennington," in *I Was Born a Slave: An Anthology of Classic Slave Narratives,* vol. 2, *1849–1866,* ed. Yuval Taylor (Chicago: Lawrence Hill Books, 1999).
2. Ibid., 139.
3. Ibid., 139–140.
4. Ibid., 140.
5. Ibid.
6. Ibid., 108.
7. See ibid., 118. This is not to say that Pennington was unable to distinguish between benign and cruel masters. He wrote that the last master he had had had not been the most cruel. Pennington's intent was to "bear witness" to the cruelty of the *system,* not to the kindness or cruelty of an individual master. Other abolitionists, such as Frederick Douglass, attested to the fact that a particular master was kind (see also ex-slave

testimonies from *Bullwhip Days: The Slaves Remember; An Oral History*, ed. James Mellon (New York: Grove Press, 1988).

8. Pennington, "The Fugitive Blacksmith," 128.
9. Ibid., 134.
10. Ibid., 141.
11. Ibid., 108.
12. Ibid., 111.
13. Ibid., 109.
14. Ibid., 108.

6. Henry Highland Garnet

1. Earl Ofari, *"Let Your Motto Be Resistance": The Life and Thought of Henry Highland Garnet* (Boston: Beacon Press, 1972), 4. Many of the black leaders who were to play a prominent role in the antislavery movement received fundamental instruction in schools organized by blacks for their own advancement.
2. Ibid., 5.
3. Ibid., 5-6.
4. Ibid., 6.
5. Ibid., 7. Many black abolitionists voiced this same sentiment. One example is Frederick Douglass, who delivered the address "What to the Slave Is the Fourth of July?" at a meeting of the Antislavery Society in Rochester, New York, in 1852.
6. Ibid.
7. Ibid.
8. Ibid., 12, 13.
9. Ibid., 14. There were other concerns of this splinter group, including their dislike of Garrison's high-handedness and his insistence upon including other causes with the antislavery society.
10. Ibid., 24.
11. Henry Highland Garnet, "An Address to the Slaves of the United States of America, Buffalo, New York, 1843," in "Appendix of Selected Speeches and Writings of Henry Highland Garnet," in Ofari, *"Let Your Motto Be Resistance,"* 144.
12. Ibid., 146.
13. Ibid.
14. Ibid., 147.
15. Ibid.
16. Ibid.
17. Ibid., 148.
18. Ibid.
19. Ibid.
20. Ibid., 148-49.
21. Ibid., 150.

22. Ibid.
23. Ibid.
24. Ibid., 151.
25. In his slave narrative Frederick Douglass also makes reference to the famous ultimatum of Patrick Henry (see Douglass, "Narrative of the Life of Frederick Douglass," in *I Was Born a Slave: An Anthology of Classic Narratives,* vol. 1, *1772–1849,* ed. Yuval Taylor (Chicago: Lawrence Hill Books, 1999), 576.
26. Garnet, "An Address to the Slaves of the United States of America," 152.

7. Samuel Ringgold Ward

1. Samuel Ringgold Ward, *Autobiography of a Fugitive Negro: His Anti-slavery Labours in the United States, Canada, and England* (1855; reprint, Eugene, OR.: Wipf and Stock Publishers, 2000), 26.
2. Ibid., 49.
3. Ibid., 37.
4. Ibid., 28.
5. Ibid., 29.
6. Ibid., 30.
7. Ibid., 37–38.
8. Ibid., 39.
9. Ibid.
10. Ibid., 41.
11. Ibid., 41–42.
12. Ibid., 42.
13. Ibid.
14. Ibid., 65–66.
15. Ibid., 64.
16. Ibid., 65.
17. Ibid., 67.
18. Ibid., 68.
19. Ibid., 69
20. Ibid., 70–71.
21. Ibid., 71.
22. Ibid.
23. Ibid., 72.
24. Ibid., 73–74.
25. Ibid., 74.
26. Ibid.
27. Ibid., 75.
28. Ibid.
29. Ibid.
30. Ibid., 76.

31. Ibid., 77.
32. Ibid., 83.
33. Ibid., 42.
34. Ibid., 43.
35. Ibid., 84.
36. Ibid.
37. Ibid., 86.
38. Ibid., 87.
39. Ibid.
40. Ibid., 88.
41. Ibid., 95.
42. Ibid., 101.
43. Unscrupulous persons could make a false claim that a black person was a runaway slave and that person would be captured and "returned" to slavery.
44. Ward, *Autobiography of a Fugitive Negro*, 121.
45. Ibid.

8. Black Abolitionism as a Quest for Human Dignity

1. David Walker, *Appeal to the Coloured Citizens of the World, But in Particular, and Very Expressly, to Those of the United States of America* (Baltimore, MD: Black Classic Press, 1993), 63.
2. James W. C. Pennington, "The Fugitive Blacksmith; or, Events in the History of James W. C. Pennington," in *I Was Born a Slave: An Anthology of Classic Slave Narratives,* vol. 2, *1849–1866,* ed. Yuval Taylor (Chicago: Lawrence Hill Books, 1999), 149.
3. Samuel Ringgold Ward, *Autobiography of a Fugitive Negro: His Antislavery Labours in the United States, Canada, and England* (1855; reprint, Eugene, OR: Wipf and Stock Publishers, 2000), 78.
4. See Henry Highland Garnet, "An Address to the Slaves of the United States of America, Buffalo, New York, 1843," in Earl Ofari, *"Let Your Motto Be Resistance": The Life and Thought of Henry Highland Garnet* (Boston: Beacon Press, 1972), 151.
5. See Ward, *An Autobiography of a Fugitive Negro,* 67.
6. Garnet, "An Address to the Slaves of the United States of America," 145.
7. Ibid.
8. Pennington, "The Fugitive Blacksmith," 110.
9. Walker, *Appeal,* 27.
10. Ibid., 29.
11. Ibid., 30.
12. Ward, *An Autobiography of a Fugitive Negro,* 37.
13. Ibid.
14. See ibid., 38.

15. Ibid., 39.

16. See ibid., 28.

17. Ibid., 354.

9. White Supremacy

1. Barry N. Schwartz and Robert Disch, *White Racism: Its History, Pathology and Practice* (New York: Dell Publishing, 1970), 14.

2. George M. Fredrickson, *The Black Image in the White Mind: The Debate on Afro-American Character and Destiny, 1817–1914* (Hanover, NH: Wesleyan University Press, 1971), 43.

3. Fredrickson, *The Black Image in the White Mind*, 43.

4. Dwight Lowell Dumond, *Antislavery Origins of the Civil War in the United States* (Ann Arbor, MI: University of Michigan Press, 1959), 2.

5. See ibid., 14.

6. Joe R. Feagin, *Racist America: Roots, Current Realities, and Future Reparations* (New York: Routledge, 2000), 11.

7. Ibid.

8. Ibid., 13.

9. Don E. Fehrenbacher, *The Dred Scott Case: Its Significance in American Law and Politics* (1978; New York: Oxford University Press, 2001), 12.

10. Cornel West, *The Cornel West Reader* (New York: Basic *Civitas* Books, 1999), 55.

11. Ibid.

12. Ibid.

13. Ibid., 71.

14. Ibid., 75.

15. Ibid., 71.

16. See ibid., 70–76.

17. Ibid., 79.

18. See ibid., 79–84.

19. Mia Bay, *The White Image in the Black Mind: African-American Ideas about White People, 1830–1925* (New York and Oxford: Oxford University Press, 2000), 14.

20. Ibid.

21. Fredrickson, *The Black Image in the White Mind*, 44. Fredrickson's summary of Thomas R. Dew's views is based on "Professor Dew on Slavery," *The Pro-Slavery Argument* (Charleston, 1852). Dew's essay was originally published as *Review of the Debate of the Virginia Legislature of 1831 and 1832.*

22. Ibid., 44–45.

23. Ibid., 46. According to Fredrickson, a "traditional quasi-environmentalist assumption" was that differences between the races could be, in some measure, ascribed to factors of climate, state of society, and manner of living (see ibid., 2). This environmentalist view differed from

the view of those who contended that the differences between the races were innate and largely immutable.

24. Ibid., 46.

25. Ibid.

26. George McDuffie, quoted in ibid.

27. Ibid., 47.

28. Ibid.

29. Ibid.

30. Ibid., 48.

31. Frederickson, *The Black Image in the White Mind*, 49.

32. Ibid.

33. Ibid.

34. Ibid.

35. Ibid., 50.

36. Bay, *The White Image in the Black Mind*, 31.

37. Ibid.

38. George M. Fredrickson, *White Supremacy: A Comparative Study in American and South African History* (New York: Oxford University Press, 1981), 153. Fredrickson gives as examples the riots that were set off in New York in 1834 and in Philadelphia in 1838 over interracial antislavery activity.

39. Bay, *The White Image in the Black Mind*, 31.

40. Fredrickson, *The Black Image in the White Mind*, 51.

41. Ibid. Taken from the *Liberator*, April 26, 1860.

42. Fredrickson, *The Black Image in the White Mind*, 52.

43. Ibid.

44. Ibid., 53, 54.

45. Ibid., 54.

46. Ibid., 53–54, 85.

47. Ibid., 57–58.

48. Ibid.

49. See Fredrickson, *White Supremacy*, 141.

50. Ibid., 151.

51. Ibid.

52. Ibid., 151–52.

53. Fredrickson, *The Black Image in the White Mind*, 71.

54. Ibid., 90.

55. Ibid.

56. Ibid., 91.

57. Ibid.

58. Ibid.

59. Ibid., 131–32.

60. Ibid., 132–33.

61. Ibid., 133.

62. Ibid., 133–34. Fredrickson cites Eugene H. Berwanger, *The Frontier against Slavery: Western Anti-Negro Prejudice and the Slavery Extension Controversy* (Urbana, IL: University of Illinois Press, 1967), 44–59.

63. Ibid., 133–35.

64. Ibid., 135.

65. Ibid., 136.

66. Ibid., 135–37.

67. Ibid., 138–39.

68. Ibid., 139.

69. Ibid., 140.

70. Ibid., 139–41.

71. Ibid., 140.

72. Ibid., 1, 141–45.

73. Ibid., 145–47.

74. Ibid., 148–49.

75. Bay, *The White Image in the Black Mind*, 14.

76. Robert William Fogel and Stanley L. Engerman, *Time on the Cross: The Economics of American Negro Slavery* (New York: W. W. Norton, 1989), 216.

77. Fredrickson, *White Supremacy*, 151.

78. Schwartz and Disch, *White Racism*, 21–22.

79. Esther M. Douty, *Forten, the Sailmaker: Pioneer Champion of Negro Rights* (Chicago: Rand McNally, 1968), 101–2.

80. Ibid., 102.

81. Charlotte Forten Grimke, *The Journals of Charlotte Forten Grimke*, ed. Brenda S. Stevenson (New York: Oxford University Press, 1988), 139–40.

82. Ibid., 140.

83. Ibid.

84. Ibid.

85. Sarah L. Forten, quoted in *We Are Your Sisters: Black Women in the Nineteenth Century*, ed. Dorothy Sterling (New York: W. W. Norton, 1984), 124.

86. Sterling, *We Are Your Sisters*, 115.

87. Clarissa C. Lawrence, quoted in ibid., 116–17.

88. Maria W. Stewart, *Meditations from the Pen of Maria W. Stewart* (Washington, DC: Garrison and Knap, 1879), 66.

89. Ibid.

90. Ibid., 25.

91. Ibid., 63.

92. Ibid., 67–73.

93. Frederick Douglass, "An Address to the Colored People of the United States," in *Frederick Douglass: Selected Speeches and Writings*, ed. Philip S. Foner (Chicago: Lawrence Hill Books, 1999), 121.

NOTES TO PAGES 119-28

94. Frederick Douglass, "Narrative of the Life of Frederick Douglass, an American Slave," in *I Was Born a Slave: An Anthology of Classic Slave Narratives*, vol. 1, *1772-1849*, ed. Yuval Taylor (Chicago: Lawrence Hill Books, 1999), 566.

95. Ibid., 570.

96. Ibid., 582.

97. Douglass, "An Address to the Colored People of the United States," 117-18.

98. Ibid., 120.

10. The Specter of Racism Infects Abolitionism

1. Dorothy Meserve Kunhardt and Philip B. Kunhardt Jr., *Twenty Days* (Secaucus, NJ: Castle Books, 1965), 59.

2. Louis Filler confirms this when he writes, "If Negroes emphasized action more than creed, white antislavery workers did the opposite" (Louis Filler, *The Crusade against Slavery 1830-1860*, rev. ed. [New York: Harper & Row, 1960], 23).

3. Thomas E. Drake, *Quakers and Slavery in America* (New Haven, CT: Yale University Press, 1950), 6-7.

4. Ibid., 14.

5. Ibid., 15.

6. Benjamin Quarles, *Black Abolitionists* (New York: Oxford University Press, 1969; reprint, Cambridge, MA: Da Capo Press, 1991), 10.

7. Ibid., 9-11.

8. Ibid., 11.

9. Ibid. In direct contrast, later abolitionists favored uncompensated emancipation, holding that if anyone deserved payment, it was the slave (see ibid., 14).

10. Ibid., 15.

11. Dwight Lowell Dumond, *Antislavery Origins of the Civil War in the United States* (Ann Arbor, MI: University of Michigan Press, 1959), 17.

12. Ibid.

13. Ibid., 17-18.

14. Jane H. and William H. Pease, *They Who Would Be Free: Blacks' Search for Freedom, 1830-1861* (New York: Atheneum, 1974), 3.

15. Ibid., 3-4.

16. Ibid., 4.

17. Ibid.

18. Ibid., 3-4.

19. Ibid.

20. Ibid.

21. Ibid., 5-8.

22. Ibid., 10.

23. Ibid., 11.

24. Ibid., 12.

25. Douglas M. Strong defines ecclesiastical abolitionism as "a movement among evangelical activists to withdraw from their denominations and to reorganize themselves into independent, locally controlled antislavery congregations." Ecclesiastical abolition has also been referred to as antislavery church reform (see Douglas M. Strong, *Perfectionist Politics: Abolitionism and the Religious Tensions of American Democracy* [Syracuse, NY: Syracuse University Press, 1999], 2).

26. Pease and Pease, *They Who Would Be Free*, 12.

27. Ibid., 12–13.

28. Shirley J. Yee, *Black Women Abolitionists: A Study in Activism, 1828–1860* (Knoxville, TN: University of Tennessee Press, 1992), 2–3.

29. Ibid., 6.

30. Ibid. Henry Mayer, in his biography of Garrison, suggests that the breach with Douglass had more to do with personality differences than with any perception of racism on Garrison's part (see Henry Mayer, *All on Fire: William Lloyd Garrison and the Abolition of Slavery* [New York: St. Martin's Griffin, 2000], 372–74).

31. George M. Fredrickson, *White Supremacy: A Comparative Study in American and South African History* (New York: Oxford University Press, 1981), 152.

32. Ibid.

33. Ibid.

34. Ibid., 156.

35. George M. Fredrickson, *The Black Image in the White Mind: The Debate on Afro-American Character and Destiny, 1817–1914* (Hanover, NH: Wesleyan University Press, 1971), 101.

36. Ibid.

37. Ibid.

38. Ibid., 107. Although Fredrickson used the UK term *racialism*, I use the American *racism* in referring to this concept.

39. Ibid., 102.

40. Charles Stuart, quoted in ibid., 103.

41. Fredrickson, *The Black Image in the White Mind*, 104.

42. Ibid., 107.

43. Lydia Maria Child, quoted in ibid., 107.

44. Fredrickson, *The Black Image in the White Mind*, 108–9.

45. Ibid., 109.

46. Ibid., 110–11.

47. Ibid., 115.

48. Ibid., 125.

49. Frantz Fanon, *Toward the African Revolution: Political Essays* (New York: Grove Press, 1988), 36.

50. Fredrickson, *The Black Image in the White Mind*, 126–27.

51. Ibid., 130.

52. Ibid., 164.

53. Mia Bay, *The White Image in the Black Mind: African-American Ideas about White People, 1830–1925* (New York: Oxford University Press, 2000), 14, 19.

54. Absalom Jones and Richard Allen, quoted in ibid., 15.

55. Bay, *The White Image in the Black Mind*, 16.

56. Ibid. Quoted from "Letter on Slavery: By a Negro?" (1789), in *Racial Thought in America: A Documentary History*, vol. 1, *From the Puritans to Abraham Lincoln*, ed. Louis Ruchames (Amherst, MA: University of Massachusetts Press, 1969), 201.

57. Bay, *The White Image in the Black Mind*, 20.

58. Ibid., 32.

59. Theodore S. Wright, quoted in ibid.

60. Quarles, *Black Abolitionists*, viii.

61. Ibid.

62. Ibid., 30.

63. Ibid., 32.

64. Ibid., 31–32, 38. Quarles cites the example of the burning down of the newly completed Pennsylvania Hall in Philadelphia in 1838 because the Second Antislavery Convention of American Women had convened there. The convention had been interracial.

65. Ibid., 47–48.

66. Ibid., 48–49.

67. Ibid., 49.

68. Ibid., 50.

69. Pease and Pease, *They Who Would Be Free*, 14, 15.

70. Ibid., 14.

71. Quarles, *Black Abolitionists*, 53.

72. Ibid., 54.

73. Ibid., 56.

74. Pease and Pease, *They Who Would Be Free*, 13–14.

75. Ibid., 13.

76. Ibid., 16.

77. Strong, *Perfectionist Politics*, 134.

78. Ibid.

79. Gerald Sorin, *Abolitionism: A New Perspective* (New York: Praeger Publishers, 1972), 17.

80. Ibid., 19.

81. Ibid., 37.

82. Ibid., 109.

83. Herman E. Thomas, *James W. C. Pennington: African American Churchman and Abolitionist* (New York: Garland Publishing, 1995), 111.

84. James McCune Smith, quoted in Pease and Pease, *They Who Would Be Free*, 91.

85. James McCune Smith, *Colored American*, May 18, 1838, cited in Carleton Mabee, *Black Freedom: The Nonviolent Abolitionists from 1830 through the Civil War* (New York: Macmillan, 1970), 106.

86. William Whipper, *National Reformer*, February 1839, cited in Sorin, *Abolitionism*, 111.

87. Sorin, *Aobolitionism*, 17.

11. The Quest Unfulfilled

1. Mark 9:29. The disciples are unable to cast out demons that had afflicted a young boy. The disciples bring the boy to Jesus, who heals him. When the disciples ask why they were unable to exorcise the demons, Jesus responds that this kind of demon can be cast out only "by prayer and fasting." The allusion is a way of reflecting upon the difficulty of eradicating white supremacy in the United States.

2. W. E. B. Du Bois, *The Souls of Black Folk* (1903; reprint, New York: Penguin Books, 1996), 1, 5.

3. George D. Kelsey, *Racism and the Christian Understanding of Man* (1962; reprint, Eugene, OR: Wipf and Stock Publishers, 2001), 27.

4. James H. Evans Jr., *We Have Been Believers: An African-American Systematic Theology* (Minneapolis: Fortress Press, 1992), 106.

5. Ibid., 15.

6. James H. Cone, *A Black Theology of Liberation*, 2nd ed. (Maryknoll, NY: Orbis Books, 1986), 84.

7. Ibid., xv.

8. Ibid., 87.

9. Ibid., 85.

10. Ibid.

11. Ibid., 87.

12. Ibid., 85, 87.

13. Du Bois, *The Souls of Black Folk*, 7.

14. Courtland Milloy, "Cash Alone Can Never Right Slavery's Wrongs," *The Washington Post*, August 18, 2002.

15. Conrad Worrill, quoted in ibid.

16. Du Bois, *The Souls of Black Folk*, 11.

17. Raimond Gaita, *A Common Humanity: Thinking about Love and Truth and Justice* (New York: Routledge, 2000), xx.

Bibliography

Bay, Mia. *The White Image in the Black Mind: African-American Ideas about White People, 1830-1925.* New York: Oxford University Press, 2000.

Cone, James H. *A Black Theology of Liberation.* 2nd ed. Maryknoll, NY: Orbis Books, 1986.

Davis, David Brion. *The Problem of Slavery in the Age of Revolution (1770-1823).* Ithaca, NY: Cornell University Press, 1975.

———. *The Problem of Slavery in Western Culture.* New York: Oxford University Press, 1984.

Douty, Esther M. *Forten, the Sailmaker: Pioneer Champion of Negro Rights.* Chicago: Rand McNally, 1968.

Douglass, Frederick. "Narrative of the Life of Frederick Douglass, an American Slave." In *I Was Born a Slave: An Anthology of Classic Slave Narratives,* vol. 1, *1772-1849,* ed. Yuval Taylor. Chicago: Lawrence Hill Books, 1999.

———. "An Address to the Colored People of the United States." In *Frederick Douglass, Selected Speeches and Writings.* ed. Philip S. Foner. Chicago: Lawrence Hill Books, 1999.

Drake, Thomas E. *Quakers and Slavery in America.* New Haven, CT: Yale University Press, 1950.

Du Bois, W. E. B. *The Souls of Black Folk.* 1903. Reprint, New York: Penguin Books, 1996.

Dumond, Dwight Lowell. *Antislavery Origins of the Civil War in the United States.* Ann Arbor, MI: University of Michigan Press, 1959.

Elkins, Stanley M. *Slavery: A Problem in American Institutional and Intellectual Life.* 2nd edition. Chicago: The University of Chicago Press, 1968.

Erickson, Millard J. *Christian Theology.* Grand Rapids, MI: Baker Book House, 1985.

Evans, James H., Jr. *We Have Been Believers: An African-American Systematic Theology.* Minneapolis: Fortress Press, 1992.

Fanon, Frantz. *Toward the African Revolution: Political Essays.* New York: Grove Press, 1988.

Feagin, Joe R. *Racist America: Roots, Current Realities, and Future Reparations.* New York: Routledge, 2000.

Fehrenbacher, Don E. *The Dred Scott Case: Its Significance in American Law and Politics.* 1978. Oxford: Oxford University Press, 2001.

Filler, Louis. *The Crusade against Slavery 1830-1860.* Rev. ed. New York: Harper & Row, 1960.

————. *Slavery in the United States.* New Brunswick: Transaction Publishers, 1998.

Fogel, Robert William, and Stanley L. Engerman. *Time on the Cross: The Economics of American Negro Slavery.* New York: W. W. Norton, 1989).

Franklin, John Hope. *From Slavery to Freedom: A History of Negro Americans.* 5th edition. New York: Alfred A. Knopf, 1980.

Fredrickson, George M. *The Black Image in the White Mind: The Debate on Afro-American Character and Destiny, 1817-1914.* Hanover, NH: Wesleyan University Press, 1971.

————. *White Supremacy: A Comparative Study in American and South African History.* New York: Oxford University Press, 1981.

Fukuyama, Francis. *Our Posthuman Future: Consequences of the Biotechnology Revolution.* New York: Farrar, Straus and Giroux, 2003.

Gaita, Raimond. *A Common Humanity: Thinking about Love and Truth and Justice.* London: Routledge, 2000.

Grimke, Charlotte Forten. *The Journals of Charlotte Forten Grimke*, ed. Brenda S. Stevenson. New York: Oxford University Press, 1988.

Hopkins, Dwight N. *Down, Up, and Over: Slave Religion and Black Theology.* Minneapolis: Fortress Press, 2000.

Johnson, Paul. *A History of the American People.* New York: HarperCollins Publishers, 1997.

Kelsey, George D. *Racism and the Christian Understanding of Man.* 1962. Reprint, Eugene, OR.: Wipf and Stock Publishers, 2001.

Kraynak, Robert P., and Glenn Tinder, eds. *In Defense of Human Dignity: Essays for Our Times.* Notre Dame, IN: University of Notre Dame Press, 2003.

Kunhardt, Dorothy Meserve, and Philip B. Kunhardt Jr. *Twenty Days.* Secaucus, NJ: Castle Books, 1965.

Litwack, Leon F. *North of Slavery: The Negro in the Free States, 1790-1860.* Chicago: The University of Chicago Press, 1961.

Mayer, Henry. *All on Fire: William Lloyd Garrison and the Abolition of Slavery.* New York: St. Martin's Griffin, 2000.

Mellon, James, ed. *Bullwhip Days: The Slaves Remember; An Oral History.* New York: Grove Press, 1988.

Meltzer, Milton C. *Slavery: A World History.* New York: Da Capo, 1993.

Miles, Johnnie H., Juanita J. Davis, Sharon E. Ferguson-Roberts, and Rita G. Giles, eds. *Educator's Sourcebook of African American Heritage.* Paramus, NJ: Prentice Hall, 2001.

Milloy, Courtland. "Cash Alone Can Never Right Slavery's Wrongs." *The Washington Post,* August 18, 2002.

Ofari, Earl. *"Let Your Motto Be Resistance": The Life and Thought of Henry Highland Garnet.* Boston: Beacon Press, 1972.

Pease, Jane H., and William H. Pease. *They Who Would Be Free: Blacks' Search for Freedom, 1830-1861.* New York: Atheneum, 1974.

Pennington, James W. C. "The Fugitive Blacksmith; or, Events in the History of James W. C. Pennington." In *I Was Born a Slave: An Anthology of Classic Slave Narratives,* vol. 2, *1849–1866,* edited by Yuval Taylor. Chicago: Lawrence Hill Books, 1999.

Quarles, Benjamin. *Black Abolitionists.* New York: Oxford University Press, 1969. Reprint, Cambridge, MA: Da Capo Press, 1991.

Schwartz, Barry N., and Robert Disch. *White Racism: Its History, Pathology and Practice.* New York: Dell Publishing, 1970.

Sorin, Gerald. *Abolitionism: A New Perspective.* New York: Praeger Publishers, 1972.

Sterling, Dorothy, ed. *We Are Your Sisters: Black Women in the Nineteenth Century.* New York: W. W. Norton, 1984.

Stewart, Maria W. *Meditations from the Pen of Maria Stewart.* Washington, DC: Garrison and Knap, 1879.

Strong, Douglas M. *Perfectionist Politics: Abolitionism and the Religious Tensions of American Democracy.* Syracuse, NY: Syracuse University Press, 1999.

Thomas, Herman E. *James W. C. Pennington: African American Churchman and Abolitionist.* New York: Garland Publishing, 1995.

Walker, David. *The Appeal to the Coloured Citizens of the World, But in Particular, and Very Expressly, to Those of the United States of America.* Introduction by James Turner. Baltimore, MD: Black Classic Press, 1993.

Ward, Samuel Ringgold. *Autobiography of a Fugitive Negro: His Antislavery Labours in the United States, Canada, and England.* 1855. Reprint, Eugene, OR: Wipf and Stock Publishers, 2000.

West, Cornel. *The Cornel West Reader.* New York: Basic Civitas Books, 1999.

Winch, Julie. *A Gentleman of Color: The Life of James Forten.* Oxford: Oxford University Press, 2002.

Woodward, C. Vann. *The Strange Career of Jim Crow.* Commemorative edition. Oxford: Oxford University Press, 2002.

Yee, Shirley J. *Black Women Abolitionists: A Study in Activism, 1828-1860.* Knoxville, TN: University of Tennessee Press, 1992.

Zilversmit, Arthur. *The First Emancipation: The Abolition of Slavery in the North.* Chicago: The University of Chicago Press, 1967.

Index